DATE			

VIRTUOSE IN ITALY, 1600–1640

GARLAND REFERENCE LIBRARY
OF THE HUMANITIES
(VOL. 404)

VIRTUOSE IN ITALY
1600–1640
A Reference Guide

Susan C. Cook
Thomasin K. LaMay

GARLAND PUBLISHING, INC. • NEW YORK & LONDON
1984

Library of Congress Cataloging in Publication Data

Cook, Susan C.
  Virtuose in Italy, 1600–1640.

  (Garland reference library of the humanities ; v. 404)
  Includes index.
  Bibliography: p.
  1. Madrigal—17th century—History and criticism.
2. Part-songs, Italian—17th century—History and
criticism.   3. Women singers—Italy—17th century.
I. LaMay, Thomasin K.   II. Title.   III. Series.
ML2633.C66   1984   784.1'2'00945   82-49141
ISBN 0-8240-9138-8

Printed on acid-free, 250-year-life paper
Manufactured in the United States of America

CONTENTS

FOREWORD

The present study grew out of our research at the University of Michigan on the madrigals of Claudio Monteverdi in the fall of 1979, and our attempt to form a performance group modeled on the singing ladies of Ferrara. We soon discovered a wealth of repertory suitable for performance by one to three female singers and *basso continuo*. Most of this literature is not discussed in the standard treatments of the Italian madrigal and is largely unavailable in modern editions. Our study attempts to correct this oversight and present a new perspective on this repertory. The introduction documents the tradition of female vocal ensembles and describes significant musical features of the repertory suitable for such ensembles. Important research has already been published concerning the Ferrarese *concerto delle donne*, most notably Anthony Newcomb's two volume study, *The Madrigal at Ferrara, 1579-1597* (Princeton: Princeton University Press, 1979) and the documentary study by Elio Durante and Anna Martelloti, *Cronistoria del Concerto del Dame Principalissime di Margherita Gonzaga d'Este* (Florence: Studi per Edizioni scelte, 1979); this study only summarizes that valuable information and emphasizes developments which occurred after the demise of the Este court. The annotated bibliography lists alphabetically by composer, the various collections possibly written for female performers, and describes the salient features of each. The appendix offers further biographical information on the women who performed, and sometimes composed this repertory. It is our hope that this annotated bibliography will encourage the publication of more modern editions, the performance of this neglected repertory, and a greater awareness of the contributions made by women to western art music.

Many people have assisted us in our work, most notably Mary Grace Smith, of Garland Publishing, Inc., who first became interested in our project, and Marie Ellen Larcada and Julia Johnson, our present editors at Garland Publishing. Mr. Wallace Bjorke, director of the University of Michigan School of Music Library deserves special thanks for having allowed us to order the countless microfilms necessary to complete our study, and we are equally appreciative of Dr. Paul Boylan, Dean of the University of Michigan School of Music, and the

Danforth Foundation, who granted funding for our research in its final stages. The New-berry Library of Chicago houses a fine col-lection of 17th-century manuscripts, and we gratefully acknowledge permission to reprint an example from their collection. Three other people deserving special recognition are Prof. David Crawford of the University of Michigan and our husbands Timothy S. Mazur and Perry S. Fine, for their encouragement and support.

Susan C. Cook and Thomasin K. LaMay
Ann Arbor, Michigan 1983

4

Francesca Caccini, "Pieta mercede aita", *Il
Primo Libro delle Musiche*(1618)

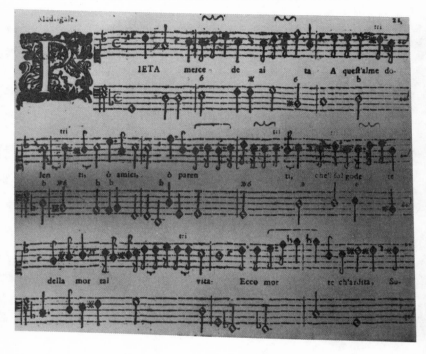

Francesca Caccini, "Pieta mercede aita", *Il Primo Libro delle Musiche*(1618)

6

Francesca Caccini, "Pieta mercede aita", *Il Primo Libro delle Musiche* (1618)

I. THE HISTORY OF THE *VIRTUOSA*[1] 1580-1640
Origin and Development to 1600

In 1581 Cavalier Grana wrote from the court of Ferrara to his Roman employer and described the new Ferrarese musical entertainment, the *concerto delle donne.*

> ...after dinner in the rooms of the Duchess he had those two ladies sing. At the end they sang a very beautiful new piece, and at that time His Highness was kind enough to call me to listen to it closely, for in truth besides being very beautiful it was decorated with such lovely and diverse *passaggi* that one could not [hope to] hear better. 2

The singing ladies of Ferrara, or *concerto delle donne*, was the unique musical creation of the Este Duke, Alfonso II. The Ferrarese court of the Este family was well-known for its artistic patronage. From the time of Isabella d'Este, in the early 16th century, Ferrara vied with Mantua as the center for new developments and innovations in the Italian madrigal.

Alfonso II created this new musical group in honor of his third wife, Margherita

Gonzaga of Mantua, whom he married in 1579. Alfonso was pleased with the prospects for his new marriage and had been given en- couragement by a French astrologer that this marriage would produce the long-awaited Este heir.[3] Margherita was a vivacious, intel- ligent woman, with a developed musical taste from her own Mantuan background. The *concer- to delle donne* was a fitting tribute to the young Duchess, and from its inception, the *concerto delle donne* became part of the high- ly prized and private musical life of the Ferrarese court, the *musica secreta*. Perfor- mances of the *musica secreta* took place in the Este apartments, and the audience con- sisted of the immediate family, high members of the court, and visiting dignitaries, thus insuring a learned audience worthy of the more sophisticated musical fare.

Ferrara, as well as other Italian courts, had groups of singing ladies before 1580. These groups were usually composed of ladies of the court who sang for their own enjoyment and for the pleasure of their employer and peers in addition to their regular duties as members of the court. But the revolutionary feature of the *concerto delle donne* of the 1580s was the professional

nature of the women involved.[4]   The members
of the new *concerto* owed their court appoint-
ments and status not to their birth but to
their talent as singers. All four members of
the Ferrarese *concerto* were of middle class
or artistic birth. They were made ladies in
waiting to Duchess Margherita, clothed,
housed, fed, provided with a salary and substantial dowry, and jealously guarded as
court treasures, all because they sang so
beautifully.

The first two members of the *concerto*,
Laura Peverara and Anna Guarini, were brought
to the court in 1580, and they were performing on a regular basis by spring of 1581.[5]
They were joined by Tarquinia Molza in 1582
and later by Livia d'Arco in 1583. Little is
known of Guarini and d'Arco, but Peverara and
Molza were quite famous in their day.

Anna Guarini, daughter of the poet Giovanni Battista Guarini, was of artistic
birth, and she played the lute as well as
sang.   She appears to have remained and performed at Ferrara for the rest of her life,
until her death in 1598 at the hands of her
husband, a gentleman of the court, who mur-
dered her presumably for reasons of adultery.

Livia d'Arco was the only member of the original *concerto* who both possessed a background of minor nobility and came to the Ferrarese court as part of Margherita's original entourage. Though arriving early at the court, she did not participate in the *concerto* until later, perhaps indicating that she required several years of training before joining the other *virtuose*.

Laura Peverara, from a Mantuan merchant family, was the performer most highly prized by the Duke who personally sent for her from Mantua in 1580. The poet Tasso, also connected with the Ferrarese court, fell in love with Peverara, wrote some 75 poems dedicated to her, and compiled two madrigal anthologies in her honor. The anthologies, *Il Lauro secco*(1582) and *Il Lauro verde*(1583) contained works for five and six voices often written especially for Peverara by such composers as Philippe de Monte, Luca Marenzio, and Giaches de Wert. The number of well-known madrigal composers who contributed to these volumes indicates the highly esteemed place and far-reaching influence Peverara had as a performer in the Ferrarese court. Peverara remained with the *concerto* until the dissolution of the Este court in 1597, and evidence indicates that she continued to live and perform in Ferrara until her death in 1601.[6]

Niece of the poet Francesco Maria Molza, Tarquinia Molza came from Modena, where she was known for her accomplishments as a singer, viola player, lutenist and poet. While at Ferrara, Molza fell in love with the Mantuan court composer Giaches de Wert, a respected musician who lacked court status. When the affair became public in 1589, the impropriety of a romance between such unequals caused the Duke to ask Molza to leave the court. Molza returned to Modena where she became even more famous and attracted her own court. She was given Roman citizenship, the first woman to receive this honor, and continued to live and work in Modena until her death in 1617.[7]

Luzzasco Luzzaschi (1545 - 1607) was the foremost male musician employed by Alfonso's court and the leading composer for the *concerto delle donne*. Luzzaschi, as *maestro di cappella* for Alfonso II, was in charge of the *musica secreta*, oversaw the practise and performance of the *concerto*, and served as their harpsichord accompanist. Other composers wrote with the *concerto* in mind, most notably

Marenzio in his first book of madrigals for six voices(1581) and Wert in his eighth book of madrigals for five voices(1586). Both of these collections are dedicated to the Ferrarese ladies and feature three prominent soprano parts which are often set off from the lower voices. Such publications suggest that the members of the *concerto* performed in larger mixed ensembles as part of their professional duties. Luzzaschi's *Madrigali per cantare, et sonare a uno, e doi e tre soprani*(1601) contains examples of music for which the *concerto* was most famous: solos, duets and trios, composed with extensive ornamentation in the voice parts and written-out harpsichord accompaniment.[8] Luzzaschi's collection of three solos, four duets, and five trios reveals the virtuosic capabilities of these professional Ferrarese singers.

The works in Luzzaschi's collection typically contrast sections of homophony with sections of florid ornamentation. The ornamentation consists of runs, often spanning more than an octave, turns, repeated figures, and written-out trills. "O dolcezz'amarissime d'amore", the first piece for three sopranos in the collection, opens with all three voices in slow-moving homophony.

The second phrase of text is treated imitatively, and then a homophonic texture returns before each voice is ornamented. The ornamental passages combine two and three voices in separate florid lines, and single out each voice for the special treatment. The ornamentation often underscores a particularly telling word in the text, and it is usually most elaborate before the final cadence.

O che' fie- ro nemi- — — —

— — — — Co

The above example, from "O dolcezz'amarissime d'amore", is typical of Luzzaschi's ornamentation. The line occurs in the uppermost soprano part, midway through the piece, and it acts as a florid counterpoint to the two homophonic vocal parts below. Luzzaschi's harpsichord accompaniment is chordal and doubles the voice

parts almost exactly, except in the ornamented sections, where the harpsichord part
is simplified.

Contemporary accounts of *concerto* performances describe various aspects of the
ladies' virtuosity. Most writers recount
performances of solos, duets, and trios with
written-out ornamental passages, as in Luzzaschi's collection, and many remark on the
Duke's great fondness for the *concerto*.[9] Besides descriptions of the *concerto* in court
correspondence and in the dedications to
madrigal publications, two other famous
treatises of the late 16th century and early
17th century describe the three singing
ladies.

Hercole Bottrigari's *Il Desiderio*(1594),
a discussion of 16th-century musical practise
in general, and Ferrarese musical life in
particular, is written in the form of a
dialogue between two fictional characters,
Gratioso Desiderio and Alemanno Benelli. The
main focus of the discussion concerns instrumental ensemble practise, so the *concerto*
is mentioned only in passing, but both
speakers know the *concerto* by reputation, if
not from personal experience. Benelli

speaks:

> those three ladies, rath-
> er those three true and
> living images of the
> Graces...I have been con-
> ceded more than once
> (thanks to the great
> kindness and generosity
> of their Serene Highnes-
> ses) the grace of both
> seeing and hearing
> them. 10

Vincenzo Giustiniani's *Discorso sopra la musica*(1628) is a much later source and refers to the *concerti* of both Ferrara, and its later imitation in Mantua, as important historical influences on the development of the new florid style of singing, which he claims spread from Northern Italy to Rome. Giustiniani's description of the *concerto* gives a clear picture of the sophisticated and highly professional nature of their performances.

> The ladies of Ferrara and
> Mantua were highly com-
> petent...they moderated
> or increased their
> voices, loud or soft,
> heavy or light, according
> to the demands of the
> piece. They were sing-
> ing; now slow, breaking
> off with sometimes a
> gentle sigh, now singing

> long passages legato or
> detached, now groups, now
> leaps, now with long
> trills, now with short,
> and again with sweet run-
> ning passages sung soft-
> ly...They accompanied the
> music and the sentiment
> with appropriate facial
> expressions, glances and
> gestures, with no awkward
> movements of the mouth or
> hands or body which might
> not express the feeling
> of the song. 11

Since the *concerto*, as part of the Ferrarese *musica secreta*, performed for all
visiting dignitaries, its popularity spread,
and by the late 1580s, imitations of the *concerto* existed in Florence, Rome, Mantua, and
a second *concerto* was begun in Ferrara.[12]
Each of these new *concerti* employed their own
professional female singers. Notable female
singers from this time include Caterina Mar-
tinelli(1589-1608), Lucia Caccini (fl. 1590),
wife of the composer Giulio Caccini, and her
daughters Settimia(1591-c.1638) and Frances-
ca(1587-c.1640), and the famous Roman soprano
and lutenist Vittoria Archilei (1550 - 1620).

Archilei, nicknamed *La Romanina*, was a
member of both the Florentine and the Roman
concerti, and she spent most of her life in

the employ of the Medici family. The composers Peri, Caccini and Sigismondo d'India
all praised her singing, and Marenzio's
second book of madrigals for six voices(1584)
contains a work "Cedan l'antiche tue" which
refers to Archilei and her Roman birthplace.
Giustiniani's *Discorso* credits Archilei with
originating "the true method of singing for
females" and spreading the new florid and
virtuosic singing style.[13]

The remaining topic in the history and
development of the early *virtuosa* is training: how and where did this new class of
professional female singers learn their art
in a society which still largely excluded
women from any professional careers? All
three members of the original *concerto* arrived in Ferrara as middle-aged women who had
already made some name for themselves as performers. Possibly the women from artistic
backgrounds, such as Molza and Guarini,
received their instruction from male
musicians of their societal class who were
either family friends or who shared the same
family employer. Women, like Peverara, from
more prosperous backgrounds may have been allowed to study with a professional male
musician. But where did other women, such as

Martinelli and Archilei, receive the kind of professional training which enabled them to perform the sophisticated repertory of the *virtuosa*? One answer may be the Roman Catholic convent.

From a biased 20th-century perspective, Renaissance convents are often portrayed as little better than dumping grounds for women who either could not function or had no place within their own society. Typically these women were the abandoned, widowed, or daughters from large families unable to afford extra dowries. Though perhaps with some basis in fact (certainly the tragic experience of Margherita Farnese gives credence to that view) such an appraisal is still one-sided. For some women, convents offered an alternative to the traditional role of wife and mother, and gave them the opportunity to pursue the scholarly activities traditionally associated with monastic life: Biblical and theological studies, teaching, and the arts. With the exception of liturgical celebrations requiring an ordained priest, all religious activities were tended to from within the confines of the convent. Convents operated as separate communities, and its members not only produced their own food and carried on their own religious instruction, but also supplied all the music needed for their ecclesiastical life. It is very likely that a woman with musical talent could have found within the convent the opportunity to develop her art and the chance to pass on her knowledge to others.

Such a supportive musical environment must have existed at the Ferrarese convent of S. Vito. Descriptions of the musical performances of the nuns of S. Vito are found in Bottrigari (*Il Desiderio*) and Artusi (*L'Artusi overo delle imperfettioni della moderna musica*), and they were known to many composers of the 16th and 17th centuries. Bottrigari discusses, at some length and in detail, the musical expertise of a group of S. Vito nuns, the *concerto grande*. The *concerto grande* was a special instrumental and vocal ensemble of twenty-three nuns who performed for special church and city occasions. Included in the *concerto grande* of Bottrigari's time was the composer Vittoria Aleotti (c.1570 - 1646), who changed her name to Raffaella upon entering the convent, and was the daughter of Alfonso d'Este's architect Giovanni Battista Aleotti. Aleotti, an organist, became the *maestra de concerto*,

the director of the *concerto grande*. Bottrigari speaks with great respect for the
maestra and the professional quality of her
concerto:

>...the most sweet harmony
>which resounds in those
>angelic voices, and those
>instruments played with
>such judgement and dis-
>cretion. 14

The performers of the cornetti and trom-
bones merited special praise by Bottrigari,
due to the difficulty of the instruments and
the rarity of their performance by women.
Signor Benelli, the "questioner" in *Il
Desiderio*, admits his astonishment at the
musical talents of the nuns, and addresses
the issue of their musical training:

>who instructed them in
>the beginning? It must
>be necessary if one
>wishes to maintain, if
>not to increase the
>bright splendor of musi-
>cal concerts, that there
>be someone who looks
>after it, and is intel-
>ligent and expert enough
>to instruct. 15

To which Signor Desiderio responds:

>that same nun [Raffaella
>Aleotti] who is director

> of the *concerto* is also
> Maestra of all beginners
> both in singing and in
> playing. 16

Even though Aleotti's talents as *maestra*
are lauded by Bottrigari, it is unlikely that
such a professional ensemble could have
developed solely during Aleotti's tenure.
The convent of S. Vito must have had an active musical life all along, which is not
surprising given its location in one of the
foremost musical cities of Renaissance Italy.
Bottrigari stated that the *concerto grande*
was not a new development, but had existed
for "tens and twenties of years", and more
importantly, no "musician or living man has
had any part in either their work or advising
them." [17] The *concerto grande* of S. Vito performed as a completely autonomous group from
the Este court, and Aleotti probably chose to
enter S. Vito not only because it was in her
hometown, but because of its musical reputation. Perhaps Aleotti received some of her
earlier musical training there as well.

Aleotti had an active musical career
through her attachment to S. Vito, and she
continued composing in addition to her work
as *maestra* and instructor of music. One of

Aleotti's five-voice madrigals first appeared
under the name Vittoria, in a special Ferrarese madrigal anthology, *Il Giardino de
musici ferrarese madrigali*, published in
1591. The inclusion of one of her works
alongside madrigals of Luzzaschi, Ludovico
Agostini, and Giulio Eremita, attests to her
reputation as a composer within her hometown.
Her first entire book of madrigals, *Ghirlanda
di Madrigali*(1593) for four voices, published
after her entrance into the convent and under
her original name, consists of eighteen
madrigals all on texts by the poet Guarini, a
personal friend of Aleotti's father. The
dedication, written by her father, mentions
the Ferrarese court-employed composers and
keyboard players Alessandro Milleville and
Ercole Pasquini, who taught Aleotti. Giovanni Battista Aleotti implies that Pasquini, so
impressed with Aleotti's talent, encouraged
him to send his daughter to the famous convent to continue her musical career.[18] Of
her music composed after her entrance into
the convent, only one collection remains, a
book of motets, *Sacrae cantiones*(1593), for
five, seven, eight, and ten voices. It is
possible that she composed more music but it
may have circulated in manuscript and is now

lost.

The convent of S. Vito and the experience of Raffaella Aleotti is not an iso-
lated musical occurrence. Many other examples exist which show that virtuoso performers and convent life often thrived
together. An anthology of three-part sacred
madrigals, *Tempio Armonico*(1599), published
by the Roman Counter-Reformation composer
Giovenale Ancina makes reference in the
dedication to the nuns of the Neapolitan convent of S. Martino, and its founder Sister
Orsola Benincasa. Ancina describes Benincasa's nuns as singing like "angels of
paradise", and Sister Giovanna Sancia, a
Spaniard, as "a Neapolitan Siren."[19] Ancina's
anthology contains works by some of the leading Roman composers including Felice and Giovanni Francesco Anerio, Scipione Dentice,
Ruggiero Giovanelli, Luca Marenzio, and Paolo
Quagliati, indicating that these well-known
composers may also have known of the talented
Neapolitan nuns, if not having written
specifically for them.

Two other composers who wrote in the
florid style for several voices and continuo,
and were connected with convents are Caterina

Assandra (fl.c.1609 - 1622) and Lucrezia Orsina (fl.c.1623). Assandra came from the
convent of S. Agata in Lomello, near Milan.
Her only surviving publication is her second
collection of sacred motets, *Motetti*(1609),
composed for two or three voices and *basso
continuo*. Later motets appeared in two
anthologies of sacred music, *Siren coelestis*(1616) and *Promptuarii musicus concentus
ecclesiasticos*(1622). Given her lifestyle,
her works were probably written for non-
liturgical performance within her convent by
trained convent musicians, and she herself
may have been a virtuoso singer. Orsina
worked at the Bolognese convent of S. Christina, and her publication, *Componimenti
Musicali di motetti concertanti*(1623), consists of sacred works for solo or several
voices and *basso continuo*. Her works may
have also had their origins in the musical
practises of her convent.

For many talented female musicians, convents held the opportunity to continue their
musical careers, to perform, conduct, compose, and teach. In the early 17th century,
more virtuosic singing nuns appeared, and
many of them seem to have attained a secular
status and popularity on an equal with their

non-cloistered peers. With all this musical activity taking place within convent life, young women, whether planning to take final vows or not, may have studied with convent performers and gone on to have careers as professional singers. The secular cult of the *virtuosa*, nurtured under Duke Alfonso in Ferrara, may fittingly have had its entire roots in female religious communities.

All of Duke Alfonso's hopes for his third marriage came to naught, and when he died in 1597 without an heir, the Papacy dissolved the Este court, and Ferrara reverted to the control of a Roman governor. Members of the original *concerto* and its imitations in other Italian courts continued to perform the repertory, and many younger women followed in their footsteps. The increasing number of virtuoso female singers required more repertory, thus other madrigal composers took Luzzaschi's lead and began to publish their own collections. Though the Este court and its long tradition of patronage and artistic innovation no longer existed, the *concerto delle donne*, Alfonso's tribute to his young wife, with its professional female performers and virtuosic madrigal repertory, had left its mark.

Virtuoso Female Ensemble Music 1600-1640

The Este court at Ferrara set a formidable precedent for professional women vocalists. Although these ladies and their immediate imitators were the first such ensembles, a study of surviving repertory suggests that the tradition continued well into the Baroque period. Most music composed for female *virtuose* was published between 1600 and 1640. More specifically, of the 77 entries annotated for this study, 35 were published between 1600 and 1620, and 28 were published between 1621 and 1630. While only 3 collections, including Luzzaschi's *Madrigali per cantare et sonare*(1601), appeared before 1610, 11 contributions by significant composers were printed after 1630. Most of this music has gone unnoticed by performers and scholars; those works which have been explored have usually been linked to the emerging cantata style. While this association is sometimes appropriate, it does not adequately describe the abundance of music for one, two, and three sopranos which was published from 1600 to 1640.

The repertory chosen for this study focuses on the female virtuoso ensemble in

Italy during the early Baroque period. The entries do not include collections for solo voice, though solos are found in volumes for one, two, and three voices. Neither are publications of canzonettas, villanellas, or other non-virtuosic styles represented, unless such works were specifically intended for professional groups of women singers. In a number of cases, we were unable to obtain microfilms of collections which looked promising, and they had to be omitted as well. Some of the entries include music for more than three voices, or for male singers. In such cases, however, the publication contains a significant amount of virtuoso female ensemble music, and it is considered integral to this study. Similarly, there are collections omitted from this survey which include some music for *virtuose*, but which were mainly intended for other performers. Ensemble music for all voice ranges was popular during the early Baroque period, and male *castrati* also sang some of the repertory written for sopranos. This study attempts only to highlight the female *virtuose* and their music.

The primary reference source for locating extant partbooks of music was *Il Nuovo Vogel*.[20] Published in 1977, *Vogel* is an updated version of research begun during the 1890s by the German musicologist, Emil Vogel. Since his death, scholars such as Alfred Einstein, Claudio Sartori, François Lesure, and others, have augmented Vogel's findings and have published a two-volume listing of all collections of secular Italian music printed in Italy between 1500 and 1700. A third volume gives the titles of individual pieces in these collections. Using *Vogel*, we located titles which suggested that the music was composed for one, two, and three voices, or for *virtuose*. Most surviving partbooks are in European libraries, particularly in Bologna, Florence, and Rome, Italy; Oxford and London, England; and Warsaw, Poland. There is also an interesting volume containing works by several composers in the Newberry Library, Chicago.

It should be stressed that this research cannot adequately account for music which was never published; nor, unfortunately, can it describe the improvisatory skills of the women who sang and composed it upon request. The printed volumes which survive and can be described are only a partial tribute to a once-proud performance tradition, and to the women who created it.

The original Ferrarese *concerto* participated in a "secret" art, and much of the
music composed for those ladies was published
after Duke Alfonso II's death in 1597. As
the fashion for female ensembles spread, so
apparently did the demand for music. The
dedications to most collections printed after
1610 suggest that publication delays seldom
occurred, or that the music had been in cir-
culation for only a few years before it was
printed. Furthermore, such dedications often
mention specific performers for whom the
music was intended, or an event for which it
was composed. Many of the women who performed the repertory were born near or after
1600, and many may have received their instruction in part from the first generation
of "singing ladies".

The women who sang in ensembles were
usually noted soloists and composers as well.
But their reputations as *virtuose* seemed to
depend equally upon their ability to improvise and perform within a group of one or
two other singers. Adriana Basile, one of
the first women singers to gain recognition
after the Este court's demise, was born just
outside Naples in 1580 and made her debut in
that city. She was a renowned contralto, and

gained considerable attention with her performances on the harp and Spanish guitar. In
1608, Duke Vincenzo Gonzaga at Mantua em-
barked upon lengthy negotiations to secure
her for his court. He agreed to numerous
conditions and an enormous salary before
Basile consented to leave for Mantua in
1610.[21] She received far more for her services than did the composer Claudio Monteverdi, who also worked in Mantua at that time.
He attested to her ensemble performances in a
letter of June 22, 1611, written to Cardinal
Ferdinando Gonzaga:

> Every Friday evening we
> make music in the Hall of
> Mirrors. Signora Adriana
> [Basile] comes to sing in
> ensemble music and invest
> it with such power as to
> delight the senses and to
> turn the room almost into
> a new theatre. 22

This letter does not describe her performing companions, but research by Susan
Parisi suggests that there were several *virtuose* working at the court of Mantua during
this time.[23] They included Lucia and Isabella Pellizzari of Vicenza; Monteverdi's wife,
Claudia; Adriana's two sisters, Vittoria and
Margherita; Caterina Martinelli, who was al-

ready famous when she died in 1608 at the age
of 17; and Settimia Caccini, younger daughter
of Giulio, who arrived in Mantua sometime
during the fall of 1613 with her husband,
Alessandro Ghivizzani. Parisi noticed that
all these women (and also male *virtuosi*) were
paid much more than other court musicians.
The Duke must have valued his professional
staff of *virtuose* to provide such generous
financial support and living accommodations.

In a subsequent letter, Monteverdi suggested that Basile sometimes sang in an ensemble which included her two sisters, Vittoria and Margherita. He noted that all
three women were also proficient composers.
In 1616, after he had become *maestro di cappella* at S. Marco in Venice, he was requested
to provide music for the wedding of Ferdinando Gonzaga II and Caterina de Medici. The
music was for an *intermezzo*, *Le Nozze di
Tedide* (now lost), and he wrote to his
librettist, Alessandro Striggio, concerning
the project:

> When His Highness orders
> that I set it to music, I
> shall bear in mind that
> the majority of the sing-
> ing parts are deities.
> So I should like to hear

them sung really expres-
sively.   I   think   the
three sisters -- Signora
Adriana and the other two
-- could sing them and
compose them. 24

Ellen Rosand located letters in which Basile
described her own compositions,[25] although
none of them were ever published. Many of
the *virtuose* probably composed or improvised
a good deal of the music they performed, and
such expertise was part of the virtuoso ensemble tradition.

Basile and her husband, Muzio Baroni,
had two daughters Leonora(b.1611) and
Caterina(b.1613). Basile trained them both
as professional singers, and Leonora
travelled as a soloist after 1627. But she
also sang frequently with her mother and
sister.[26] Basile and her daughters left Mantua and settled in Rome in 1633, where they
gave numerous chamber concerts and enjoyed
the partronage of the Rospigliosi family.

There were noted *virtuose* in other
Italian cities who also performed in ensembles. Francesca Caccini, oldest daughter
of Giulio Caccini, was born in Florence in
1587 and worked there throughout her life.
Nicknamed *La Cecchina*, she was an ac-

complished poetess, instrumentalist, and composer, as well as *virtuosa*. She toured as a
professional singer in both Italy and France,
and performed in an ensemble in Florence.
The ensemble was described by the poet Jacopo
Cicognini(1577-1633), who sometimes provided
texts for her compositions. In 1612, he
wrote the following about an ensemble performance during Carnival season at the Pitti
Palace in Florence:

> The above-mentioned *ot-
> tavi* were composed musi-
> cally by the same women
> who sang them. The first
> was sung with her usual
> grace and angelic voice
> by Vittoria Archilei, the
> Roman; and the second
> with every supreme excel-
> lent art by the Lady Set-
> timia; and the third with
> her usual readiness and
> universal admiration by
> the Lady Francesca, both
> daughters of the most
> celebrated Giulio Romano;
> and the fourth *ottavo*
> composed by the same
> Francesca with most
> graceful and engaging
> style, united them with
> such beautiful fugues and
> ornamental passages. 27

Cicognini's description of solos by three
ladies, followed by a virtuosic ensemble

piece for all three, closely resembles the
performance practice established by Luzzaschi's *concerto*. Francesca and her sister often sang together in Florence, even after
Settimia was engaged at Mantua in 1613. Vittoria Archilei, the other woman mentioned by
Cicognini, travelled between Florence and
Rome each year. Born in 1550, Vittoria would
have been 62 at the time of this particular
performance; she was nearly 40 when the Caccini sisters were born. She was a member of
the first Florentine *concerto*, started by
Duke Francesco in 1584, and her knowledge of
the tradition must have aided in the development of Francesca's own style.

Barbara Strozzi was a well-known
Venetian *virtuosa* and composer. She was born
in 1619, probably as the illegitimate
daughter of the poet Giulio Strozzi. She was
always a member of his household, and he
eventually adopted her and made her sole
heiress of his estate.[28] Through her father,
Strozzi gained access to the intellectual
elite of Venice. That city did not sponsor a
concerto, but Giulio Strozzi arranged for his
daughter to sing at home, where she was heard
by a select audience. The composer Nicolò
Fontei (? - c.1647) composed two volumes of

Bizzarrie poetiche for her, which were published in 1635 and 1636. The first collection contains largely solo repertory, with only three pieces for soprano ensemble. But the 1636 volume includes numerous dialogues for the poetic characters, Tirsi and Chloris, which were written for two sopranos and *basso continuo*. This implies that once Strozzi established her reputation as a capable singer, another soprano was acquired by Giulio Strozzi to perform with her at his home.

Apparently Giulio Strozzi decided to institutionalize his daughter's performances in 1637, with the creation of the Accademia degli Unisoni. Strozzi served as mistress of ceremonies for debates on academic and frivolous subjects, and was expected to improvise songs on the daily topics for discussion.[29] The Accademia did not keep records of other women who performed there, but it is evident from descriptions of various meetings that other female singers were usually present.[30]

Strozzi also published eight volumes of music. While Ellen Rosand stresses the composer's contributions to the cantata style, she also suggests that the terms *aria* and

cantata are inadequate to describe the formal
variety of her works.[31] The title pages of
her publications advertise madrigals, ariet-
tas, arias, and cantatas, but her texts are
almost all love themes typical of "singing
ladies" material. Many of them derive or are
taken directly from madrigal poems of the
late Renaissance.

Rosand also notices that a large portion
of Strozzi's music remains textless, due to
frequent and lengthy ornamentation. Three-
quarters of her published works are for solo
soprano, but the first three volumes(1644,
1651, and 1654) concentrate on ensemble
music, including several duets and trios.
Rosand further mentions that Strozzi never
sang in opera, which for Venice, was the ob-
vious place for *virtuose* to leave their mark:

> She was a singer in Ven-
> ice, surrounded by
> librettists and im-
> presarios at a time when
> opera was the main cul-
> tural interest of a large
> segment of Venetian
> society, yet she ap-
> parently never sang in
> opera. She was a gifted
> composer with the fore-
> most opera composer of
> her day [Cavalli], yet
> she never wrote an opera.

> Despite the fact that
> those around her were
> deeply involved in public
> activity, her sphere
> seems strangely enclosed,
> insular and self-
> contained. Her academic
> performances and eight
> published volumes are es-
> sentially all we know of
> her career. 32

Venice was a prominent operatic center after 1640, yet Barbara Strozzi, *virtuosis-sima cantatrice*, specialized only in solo and ensemble chamber music. She performed privately, and with other sopranos; she composed and improvised, and the emphasis on ornamentation is unmistakable in her published scores. She was one of the last to work in the tradition of the *concerto delle donne*.

Music for the female virtuoso ensemble was not limited to the secular repertory. Collections of sacred madrigals, on both Latin and Italian texts, were published for one, two and three voices. These were as demanding as their secular counterparts, conforming to the virtuoso tradition, and were most likely intended for talented nuns. The following example, from Severo Bonini's *Affetti spirituali* (1615) and titled "Versa est", demonstrates the quality and virtuosity of the sacred repertory.

It has been suggested earlier in this study that some convents were important centers of musical training for *virtuose* during the Renaissance. There is significant evidence to suggest that this trend continued into the early 17th century. Two Roman composers, Paolo Quagliati (c.1555 - 1628) and Pietro Sabbatini (c.1600 - 1657) dedicated collections to the nuns at S. Maria Maggiore; Quagliati served as organist there from 1601 to 1628. One of his pupils, Pietro della Valle, wrote in his *Della musica dell'età nostra*, printed in 1640, that these nuns were the marvel of Rome. He also mentioned the convents of S. Lucia in Selice, S. Silvestro, Monte Magnanapoli, and S. Chiara as being institutions in or near Rome which sponsored virtuoso groups.[33] He wrote that these women had for many years "stupified the world" with their manner of singing.[34]

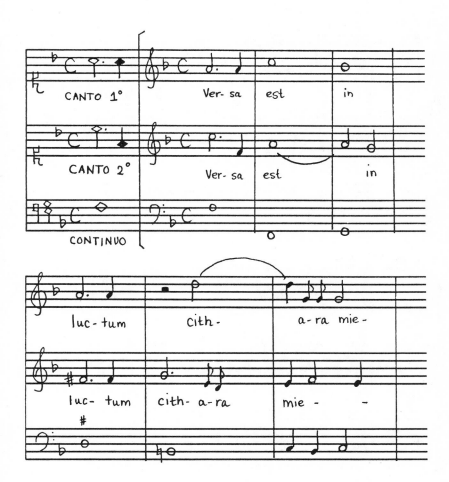

The nuns of S. Lucia in Selice gained special recognition after 1620 for the performances of Sister Anna Maria Cesi. She came from the Marchesi d'Oliveto branch of the noble Roman Cesi family, and her brothers held important government and church posts.[35] She professed to have been born in 1608, but was probably born around ten years earlier, for she was already residing at S. Lucia by 1617. Quagliati dedicated his *Affetti amorosi spirituali* to her in that year, and in 1640 Sabbatini dedicated his *Canzoni spirituali a una, due e tre voce* to her, then Donna Anna Maria Cesi Peretti. Della Valle wrote in *Della musica* that "Everyone knows

how much renown the nun at Santa Luccia in
Selice has."[36]   Her change in name later in
life, and the early age at which Cesi entered
the convent, suggest that she was sent there
precisely to study music, and not necessarily
to become a nun. Her parents could easily
have afforded to keep her at home, or provide
her with the generous dowry which they eventually offered. Cesi evidently demonstrated
musical talent at a young age. Since the
convent at S. Lucia was noted for its musical
teaching, her parents must have sent her
there to develop her skills. After she had
established herself as a *virtuosa*, Cesi was
free to leave the convent and was married.
People came from all over Italy to hear the
nuns at that convent. Before he died in
1628, Quagliati left instructions in his will
that his spinet should be offered to the
singing nuns at S. Lucia, a further sign of
admiration.[37]

The convent must have had several
capable singers who performed the routine
daily offices. Significant for this study,
though, are the numerous collections of
sacred music published for only one, two, and
three sopranos. This implies that at least
the convents mentioned by della Valle in-

cluded a virtuoso female ensemble which func-
tioned as part of, but also apart from
regular church life. For example, Sister
Anna Maria apparently performed with her two
natural sisters, Giovanna and Maddelena. The
former was also at S. Lucia, but Maddelena
was a member of S. Maria.[38] They were allowed
to sing for public audiences, not just for
church services, and they practised together.
The convents evidently coveted their *concerti
delle donne* just as did the courts.

The performance tradition for one, two,
and three women flourished well into the early Baroque era. The women who sang in *concerti* were often soloists and composers as
well, and a few, such as Settimia Caccini and
Adriana Basile, appeared in operas. But *virtuose* were still judged by their ensemble
performances, and their contemporaries attested to the significance and frequency of
those events.

The surviving repertory suggests that
there was substantial demand for virtuoso ensemble music. Such music for women emphasizes many of the features that had been
introduced by the Ferrarese *concerto*. The
format often mirrors Luzzaschi's collections:

pieces for one soprano, followed by a number
of works for two, then three voices. The
collections demonstrate a like interest in
difficult, written-out ornamentation. There
is always a *basso continuo* accompaniment, and
the texts, like Luzzaschi's, are drawn from
madrigal repertory or are imitative of it.
Even Barbara Strozzi's texts, composed mainly
by her father, are reminiscent of earlier
literature.[39] Such collections appeared as
late as the 1650s, suggesting that the tradition blended easily with the emerging Baroque
preference for duet and trio textures with
accompaniment. In fact, the Baroque trio
sonata, with its emphasis on florid upper
voices over a harmonic bass, must have
developed in part from the "three singing
ladies" repertory, which had its roots in the
late Renaissance.

NOTES

1. The Italian *virtuosa*, which denotes sex
   as well as the caliber of a performer,
   and its plural *virtuose*, were used by
   writers of the time to describe the
   female performers of a new florid style
   of vocal music. Because our study
   describes a female performance tradition, we have elected to use the
   original Italian nouns, while using the
   standard English adjectives "virtuoso"
   and "virtuosic".

2. Anthony Newcomb, *The Madrigal at Ferrara,
   1579-1597*. 2 vols. Princeton Studies in
   Music 7. (Princeton: Princeton University Press, 1980), p. 25. Prof. Newcomb
   has done the most research in the area
   of 16th-century Ferrarese musical life
   and the historical background of the
   concerto delle donne. We are greatly
   indebted to his study.

3. Newcomb, *The Madrigal at Ferrara*, I:105.

4. Newcomb, *The Madrigal at Ferrara*, I:7.

5. Newcomb, *The Madrigal at Ferrara*, I:21.

6. Newcomb, *The Madrigal at Ferrara*, I:184.

7. Carol MacClintock, *Giaches de Wert*.
   Musicological Studies and Documents 17.
   (Rome: American Institute of Musicology,
   1966), p. 46.

8. Luzzaschi's publication is now available
   in both facsimile and modern editions.
   Luzzasco Luzzaschi, *Madrigali per sonare
   et cantare*, Archivum Musicum Collana di
   Testi rari 35. (Florence: Studio per

Edizioni scelte, 1980). Adriano Cavic-
chi,   ed.   *Luzzasco   Luzzaschi,
Madrigali*. Monumenta di musica italiana
Ser. 2, Polifonia 2. (Brescia: L'Organo,
1965).

9. Newcomb's study translates many contempo-
    rary descriptions of the *concerto* found
    in private court correspondence. For
    more documentation on the *concerto* in
    the original Italian, see Elio Durante
    and Anna Martelloti, *Cronistoria del
    Concerto del Dame Principalissime di
    Margherita Gonzaga d'Este*, Archivum
    Musicum Collana di Studi A (Florence:
    Studio per Edizioni scelte, 1979). In
    addition to court correspondence and
    dedications to musical and poetic works
    which mention members of the *concerto*,
    Durante and Martelloti include reproduc-
    tions of two contemporary portraits of
    Molza from private collections.

10. Hercole Bottrigari, *Il Desiderio*, trans.
    by Carol MacClintock. Musicological
    Studies and Documents 9. (Rome: American
    Institute of Musicology, 1962), p. 58.

11. Vincenzo Giustiniani, *Il Discorso sopra
    la musica*, trans. by Carol MacClin-
    tock. Musicological Studies and Docu-
    ments 9. (Rome: American Institute of
    Musicology, 1962), p. 69.

12. Newcomb, *The Madrigal at Ferrara*, I:90.

13. Giustiniani, *Il Discorso*, p. 70.

14. Bottrigari, *Il Desiderio*, p. 58

15. Bottrigari, *Il Desiderio*, p. 60.

16. Bottrigari, *Il Desiderio*, p. 60.

17. Bottrigari, *Il Desiderio*, p. 59.

18. Emil Vogel, *Bibliografia della Musica Italiana Vocale Profana pubblicata dal 1500-1700*. 3 vols. Nuovo edizione Alfred Einstein, François Lesure, Claudio Sartori.(Pomezia: Staderini-Minkoff, 1977), I:30-31. Most of the dedication to *Ghirlanda* is reproduced here.

19. Emil Vogel, *Weltliche Vocalmusik Italiens*. 2 vols. reprint (Hildesheim: Georg Olms, 1962), II:482; "di quella dolce Sirena Napolitana detta Giovanna Sancia ... e suonando qual nuova e pura Angioletta di Paradiso."

20. Emil Vogel, *Bibliografia della Musica Italiana Vocale Profana pubblicata dal 1500-1700, op. cit.*

21. See Alessandro Ademollo, *La Bell'Adriana ed altre virtuose del suo tempo* (Citta di Castello, 1888).

22. Denis Arnold and Nigel Fortune, eds. *The Monteverdi Companion* (London: Faber and Faber, 1968), p. 35.

23. Susan Parisi, "The 'Virtuosi' at the Court of Mantua, 1600-1625", a paper given at the National Meeting of the American Musicological Society, Nov., 1979. We gratefully acknowledge receiving a copy of the paper.

24. Arnold and Fortune, eds., *The Monteverdi Companion*, p. 42.

25. Ellen Rosand, "Barbara Strozzi, *vir-*

tuosissima cantatrice: The Composer's
Voice," *Journal of the American
Musicological Society*, 31(1978), p. 254.

26. M. Alessandrini, "Una celebre cantatrice
    alla corte di Urbano VIII, Leonora
    Baroni," *Scenario*, 9(1942), p. 152.

27. Translated in: Carolyn Raney, "Francesca
    Caccini, Musician to the Medici and her
    Primo Libro" (Ph.D. diss., New York
    University, 1971), p. 44.

28. Rosand, "Barbara Strozzi," pp. 241-242.

29. Rosand, "Barbara Strozzi," pp. 244-246.

30. Rosand, "Barbara Strozzi," p. 247.

31. Rosand, "Barbara Strozzi," p. 266.

32. Rosand, "Barbara Strozzi," p. 280.

33. Pietro della Valle, "Della musica
    dell'età nostra" in Angelo Solerti, ed.,
    *Le Origini del Melodrama. Testimonianze
    dei Contemporanei* (Torino: Fratelli Boc-
    ca, 1903), pp. 148-179.

34. della Valle, "Della musica,"
    pp. 166-167; "Ha fatto piu anni stupire
    il mondo."

35. Margaret Rorke, "The Spiritual Madrigals
    of Paolo Quagliati and Antonio Cifra"
    (Ph.D. diss., University of Michigan,
    1980), pp. 43-44.

36. della Valle, "Della musica", p. 166; "La
    monaca di Santa Lucia in Silice [sic]
    ognun di quanta fama sia."

37. Rorke, "The Spiritual Madrigals", pp. 44-45.

38. Rorke, "The Spiritual Madrigals", p. 45.

39. Rosand, "Barbara Strozzi", p. 262.

Antonio Cifra, "Vostro fui vostro son e
saro", *Diversi Scherzi* (1613)

Antonio Cifra, "Vostro fui vostro son e saro", *Diversi Scherzi* (1613)

II. MUSICAL REPERTORY FOR THE FEMALE VOCAL ENSEMBLE

Roman Collections

Rome, with its dependence on church patronage rather than a single ducal court, was far from being the bastian of musical conservatism one might expect from the capital of Catholicism. Though center of the Tridentine reforms of Catholic Church music, Rome played an important part in the continued development of music for the *virtuosa*. Giustiniani in his *Discorso* spoke highly of Rome as a center of the highly developed florid singing style,[1] and many professional singers, female and male, worked and performed there. Notably the presence of Vittoria Archilei, whom Giustiniani singled out as a particularly influential performer, the composer and singer Francesca Campana, and the nuns of the convent of S. Lucia in nearby Selice, show that Rome had its own *virtuose*. Of all the collections significant to our study, 49, or almost half, were published by composers either residing in Rome or with strong Roman ties. Rather than ignoring the new interest in the female singer, Rome welcomed it enthusiastically and adapted the tradition to its own use.

The primary composers of the Roman repertory were Giovanni Francesco Anerio (c.1567 - 1630), Antonio Cifra (1584 - 1629), Paolo Quagliati (c.1555 - 1628), Raffaello Rontani (? - 1622), and Filippo Vitali (c.1590 - 1653). The bulk of their compositions appeared in publication before the 1620s. Later Roman collections often show the increased popularity of the simpler strophic aria style rather than the more typically virtuosic madrigal. Though many Roman composers favored duets for two sopranos, they typically saved their most virtuosic writing for solo works. In these solos, each phrase of text is ornamented which produces highly florid works of unrelieved difficulty. In general, the three primary features of the Roman collections are: 1. the use of sacred Italian texts, 2. the use of the male voice in three-voice textures, and 3. the practise of composing over a repeated bass pattern, or harmonic formula.

As theological hub of the Counter-Reformation movement, Rome logically became the center for increased interest in all forms of sacred music. The liturgical works of Palestrina have long been recognized as outgrowths of the Counter-Reformation spirit, but this same devotion to sacred music also stimulated the composition of spiritual madrigals, compositions which wedded texts of Catholic piety and devotion to the musical nature of the secular madrigal.[2] The 1610s and 1620s witnessed the greatest musical development of the Counter-Reformation spirit and the largest number of published collections of spiritual madrigals.[3] Of the 49 Roman collections included here, 11 feature spiritual texts demonstrating how Rome adapted the *virtuosa* to its own Counter-Reformation needs.

Spiritual madrigals most likely were performed in the same setting as secular madrigals, as part of private entertainments for wealthy families. Such religious works would have been especially appropriate during the time of Lent and Holy Week. Rome's many churches, religious academies, and *oratori* afforded a great number of opportunities for the performance of spiritual works. Roman convents, and convents in general, undoubtedly preferred performing spiritual works over secular, thereby insuring a market and audience for these compositions. Composers outside of Rome also published spiritual works for the *virtuosa* but Rome, with its Counter-Reformation fervor, produced the greatest number of such collections.

Nicolo Borboni's collection, *Musicali concenti*(1618) contains settings of both sacred and secular Italian texts. One of the most florid pieces in the collection is a solo work in two *parti* "Vergine gloriosa, di Dio figliola". The adulation and heartfelt sentiment of the text allow for ample word painting and ornamentation worthy of any professional singer.

The spiritual collection of Paolo Quagliati, *Affetti amorosi spirtuali*(1617), was dedicated to the performer Sister Anna Maria Cesi (discussed earlier in the study), who may have been the first to perform this music. Quagliati's entire collection contains settings of spiritual Italian texts for one, two, and three voices, in both the simpler *villanelle* style, and in the more virtuosic madrigal style. The texts include statements of praise, adoration, thanksgiving, and requests for mercy.

Giovanni Francesco Anerio spent most of his life in Rome and wrote much sacred music including Latin masses as well as Italian-

texted works for Filippo Neri's Oratorio,
most notably his *Teatro armonica spir-
tuale*(1619). *Selva armonica*(1617), one of
his two publications in the virtuoso style,
is a large collection of sacred texts set for
one to four voices. Included in the collection are sacred Italian, as well as Latin-
texted pieces, including a "Salve Regina" for
solo soprano. One work, "Giesu, nel tuo par-
tire", set as a duet for two sopranos or
soprano and tenor, is a dialogue between the
repenitent soul and Christ. The collection
was dedicated to Isabella Avilla.

Another particular feature of most Roman
collections is the use of a bass voice within
a three-voice texture. Roman composers were
particularly fond of duets, especially when
coupled with a repeated bass pattern (to be
discussed later.) However in three-voice
textures, the third voice appears not as in
Luzzaschi's collection, as a third soprano,
but rather as a bass.

The popular Roman three-voice *villanelle*
was typically composed with two canto voices
and a bass, without *basso continuo*.[4] The
later three-voice virtuosic repertory,
featuring florid writing and the addition of

basso continuo, may simply demonstrate a holdover from the older *villanelle* style. Rome also possessed a number of accomplished male singers, and many Roman collections contain together with music suitable for the *virtuosa*, ornamented solos for the male voice. Roman composers may have enjoyed exploiting both the high and low registers and composing for male and female professional singers.

Typically in these three-voice works, the *basso continuo* doubles the bass part, except for repeated notes or filled-in thirds. In collections where space is limited, no separate *basso continuo* part is notated, instead it must be derived from the texted, and at times figured, bass voice part. In many examples, the two upper soprano parts are more ornamented and florid than the bass line, and composers often exploit the high and low ranges by pitting the upper voices against the bass and *basso continuo*.

The third and most pervasive feature of the Roman collections is the practise of composing over bass patterns, or harmonic progressions. This compositional technique, of Renaissance origin, was probably first used for dance music. A harmonic progression became associated with a set of dance steps, or dance rhythm, and this progression was repeated with an improvised melody above as many times as necessary to complete the dance. The *passamezzo antico* and *moderno* basses probably evolved in this manner. Composers later adapted this method of generating a set of variations from a repeating harmonic theme to idiomatic instrumental and vocal composition.

Diego Ortiz's *Tratado de glosas*(Rome, 1553) contains the first instrumental compositions derived from bass patterns. The *Tratado* provides instruction in ornamentation practises and defines various kinds of music suitable for performance on the the viola da gamba. At the end of the second volume, Ortiz illustrates the different genres of viol music with a series of *recercadas* or studies including eight compositons "sobre tenores Italianos". These *recercadas* are idiomatic viol compositions built on a variety of Renaissance bass patterns, including the *folia, passamezzo antico* and *moderno* and *romanesca* basses. To perform these works, a keyboardist repeats the harmonic progression while the violist plays an ornamented line which becomes more difficult as the pattern continues.

Spanish keyboard and vihuela composers, such as Antonio de Cabezón (c.1510 - 1566) and Alonso de Mudarra (c.1510 - 1580) adapted bass patterns to their compositions as well, and the popularity of such variation sets spread to Italy. In the 16th century, the Italian keyboard composers Antonio Valente (fl.1565 - 1580) and Giovanni de Macque (c.1548 - 1614) popularized such compositions. Valente's *Intavolatura de cimbalo*(1576) contains variations on the *romanesca* bass, a pattern closely associated with the Spanish melody "O guardame las vacas". Macque was the first to use the name "ruggiero" for the pattern employed in his composition, though the progression itself had appeared unnamed in Ortiz's *Tratado*.[5] The *ruggiero* and *romanesca* basses continued to be the most popular progressions.

In the 17th century, Italian composers such as Scipione Stella (c.1559 - c.1630), Ascanio Mayone (c.1565 - 1627), Giovanni Maria Trabaci (c.1575 - 1647), and Ercole Pasquini (c.1580 - 1620) continued to compose idiomatic keyboard works on bass patterns.

The most well-known composer utilizing bass patterns was Girolamo Frescobaldi(1583-1643), notably in his four *partite* on the *romanesca*, *monicha*, *ruggiero* and *follia* (different from the *folia*) basses, originally published in the first book of toccatas and partitas of 1615. These variation sets are elaborate works with six to fourteen repetitions of the bass pattern. Frescobaldi ornaments the harmonic pattern from the outset and the succeeding repetitions provide a catalogue of variation techniques, including rapidly changing ornamentation in both hands and changes of meter. Certainly one reason for the popularity of the bass pattern variation set was the opportunity it afforded to explore the idiomatic possibilities of the instrument and to highlight the talents of a given performer.

In the early 17th century, the use of bass patterns spread to vocal music. The titles for such compositions, typically "l'aria sopra de romanesca", or "l'aria di ruggiero" may imply that these bass patterns were originally used in vocal music as schemes for improvising and performing strophic aria texts.[6] Later though, these harmonic patterns were used in vocal music as the basis for written-out compositions which made use of variation techniques as developed in the instrumental repertory. This adaptation of an instrumental technique to vocal music reverses the standard practise of vocally derived instrumental music.

The use of bass patterns in Roman vocal music appears in solo and duet works only. The three-voice Roman texture precluded the use of bass patterns as the bass voice would be relegated to doubling the bass pattern. The Roman composers typically favored the *ruggiero* bass, a pattern in the major mode, and the *romanesca* bass, a minor mode progression. The vocal composers, like their instrumental counterparts, used the repeating bass as a stable foundation from which to launch a series of variations designed to show off vocal technique and skill. It is understandable that collections of Roman music written with professional singers in mind would draw upon the virtuosic bass pattern technique. Vocal music composed over basses was not exclusively the province of Roman composers, as examples appear in non-Roman collections. Francesca Caccini's *Musiche* (1618) contains several very florid solo pieces on the *romanesca* bass, likewise

Eleuterio Guazzi's *Spiritosi affetti*(1622) contains a solo work on the *romanesca*, and a duet on the *romanesca* bass appears in Monteverdi's seventh book of madrigals(1614). But it is only in Rome that bass pattern vocal works appear with such regularity and characterize entire collections.

The compositions of the Roman composer Antonio Cifra display all three Roman features, and Cifra published an unprecedented number of collections suitable for the virtuoso performer. Cifra spent most of his life in the employ of major churches in or related to Rome. He was *maestro di cappella* at the important Counter-Reformation shrine, S. Casa di Loreto, from 1609-1622, after which he went to S. Giovanni in Laterano in Rome from 1623-1626, then returned to Loreto. Cifra was by far one of the most prolific composers of the Roman school with thirty publications of sacred works, including Latin motets, psalms and masses, and eleven secular publications.

As a secular composer, Cifra is most known for his six books of five-voice madrigals. Though often set to some of the most popular and appealing madrigal texts

("T'amo, mia vita", "Luci seren'e chiare", "O
come e gran martire"), Cifra's musical settings in Palestrinian counterpoint appear
bland and undistinguished when compared with
those of his Northern Italian contemporaries.
But this reputation for mediocrity is invalid
with regard to his compositions for one, two,
and three voices. In these eight collections, published between 1613 and 1619, Cifra
supplies solos, duets, and trios demonstrating his ability to compose in the florid
style. He also left the largest number, and
some of the finest examples of, vocal works
composed on bass patterns.

Of Cifra's eight collections, two
publications, the *Scherzi sacri* of 1616 and
1618, are entirely set to sacred texts. All
eight collections contain a variety of
styles: virtuosic solos and duets composed
without bass patterns and designated as
madrigale, solos and duets composed on bass
patterns and so designated in the *tavola*,
three-voice works in the Roman texture, and
simple homophonic pieces usually referred to
as *arie*, *canzonetti*, or *madrigaletti*. In
general, Cifra's solo works are the most
florid and vocally demanding.

The majority of Cifra's duets are composed on harmonic bass patterns. Solo works
on basses do not appear until the last two
collections, *Diversi Scherzi*(1617) and *Scherzi*(1619). Cifra favored the popular *romanesca* and *ruggiero* basses but also used the less
common *gazzella* bass, a longer minor mode
pattern. Typically Cifra repeats the bass
pattern four times, thus dividing the complete work into four stanzas. Through con-
trasts of imitative counterpoint, homophony,
and different kinds of ornamentation, the
voice parts provide a set of variations over
the bass.

"Vostro fui vostro son e saro", an "aria
de Ruggiero a due soprani", is the first duet
in Cifra's *II. Diversi Scherzi*(1613). This
duet (see facsimile, pages 50-51) is typical

of Cifra's florid style and demonstrates Cifra's subtle manipulations of the bass pattern. The *ruggiero* bass, the shortest of the
common patterns, is usually divided into four
phrases of roughly two bars each.

Cifra upsets this natural division by
repeating the last four measures of the pattern which produces a tripartite formal
scheme made up of three four-measure phrases.

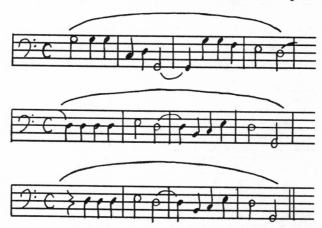

Cifra repeats this new version of the
ruggiero pattern four times with different
vocal treatment for each repetition. Cifra's
ornamentation is similar to Luzzaschi's,
favoring octave runs, and four-note repeated
patterns, and the ornamented passages are often imitative. Cifra also uses the ornament

sign for a *trillo* (t) in the upper soprano part.

The Newberry Library of Chicago owns an important source of early 17th-century Roman vocal music, a volume of eight publications bound together.[7] The title on the spine of the original vellum binding reads *Musike di Vitali ed Alteri Compositori|Roma 1620-25*. The five composers of the eight collections are Filippo Vitali (1620), Raffaello Rontani (1623, 1623, 1625), Antonio Cifra (1615), Giuseppe Olivieri (1620), Alessandro Capece (1625), and Giuseppe Giamberti (1623). All composers were connected with Rome.

In general, this Roman source contains a mixture of virtuosic works for the profes-sional singer and simpler works for the amateur. The Vitali collection contains en-tirely works of a simple, strophic nature. The three collections by Rontani are predominantly for solo voice, including vir-tuosic pieces for soprano and tenor. The Ci-fra work contains ornamented solos, bass pat-tern duets, and simpler *arie*. The large Olivieri collection, *La pastorella Armilla*, contains settings of pastoral texts in both the more virtuosic madrigal and the simpler *ariette* styles. The madrigals in the Capece collection are virtuosic works for solo and duet. And the Giamberti collection is primarily solo repertory with works for the male voice, including a baritone piece on the *romanesca* bass.

No further information is available at the Newberry Library concerning the original owner of this source, but the good condition of the volume suggests that it was a special gift or dedication collection rather than a copy for performance use. The three collections by Rontani, a composer primarily of solo repertory, further suggests that the volume belonged to a solo singer, either a professional, or perhaps an amateur of Roman nobility.

The Newberry Library volume provides a good synopsis of early 17th-century Roman vocal music. It presents examples of both virtuosic music for the professional, and simpler music for the amateur, works for both female and male voice, and pieces composed on bass patterns. The collection only lacks in the absence of works on sacred Italian texts. In all, Rome made significant contributions to the tradition of the *virtuose* by providing

singers, performance opportunities, and most
importantly, repertory.

70

Giovanni Battista da Gagliano, "Ninfe prole del ciel", *Varie Musiche*(1623)

Giovanni Battista da Gagliano, "Ninfe prole
del ciel", *Varie Musiche* (1623)

Giovanni Battista da Gagliano, "Ninfe prole
del ciel", *Varie Musiche*(1623)

The North Italian Style

There was a significant amount of inter-
action between Roman performers and composers, and those working in northern Italian
cities. Vittoria Archilei travelled frequently between Florence and Rome. The Roman
composer and keyboard artist, Girolamo Frescobaldi, worked for a time in Florence, where
he published his first and second books of
Arie musicale for one, two and three voices
in 1630. Filippo Vitali produced four
volumes of music for female ensemble which
were published in Venice, Florence and Rome.
Even Luzzaschi's *Madrigali*, specifically
designed for the Ferrarese *concerto*, was
first published in Rome in 1601. Composers,
performers, and court establishments were
aware of musical activities in other cities,
and institutions continuously vied to attract
and keep talented performers. Therefore,
composers working in the north sometimes
wrote music in the Roman style, and often
titled those collections "a la romana". Bass
patterns were used by north Italian composers, and the combination of two *virtuose*
and bass or tenor proved useful in varying
music designed to highlight the female voice.

Music written in a north Italian style differs from the Roman practise in noticeable ways. Importantly, the pieces more often conform to Luzzaschi's madrigals for three sopranos. Written-out ornamentation is primarily used to highlight certain words. The embellishments are well-spaced so several bars of expressive, non-ornamented music come between *passaggi*: in the highly virtuosic Roman style, there are few unadorned passages. Also like Luzzaschi's pieces, north Italian works employ a two- or three-voice texture where all voices are equal in melodic interest. Embellishments are passed imitatively from voice to voice, while the *basso continuo* provides the harmonic support. Each part has a similar number of ornaments, and the voices often overlap in range. Occasionally, the *basso continuo* part also includes written-out *passaggi* or scales. This is most commonly the case when the music was intended for a singer who was a skilled accompanist.

Florence was the main center for music composed and performed in the north Italian style. The Florentine court had one of the most active professional ensembles after 1610, with singers such as Francesca and Settimia Caccini, and Vittoria Archilei. Many composers provided music, including Marco da Gagliano, and his younger brother, Giovanni Battista. Marco(1582-1643) was *maestro di cappella* at the Medici Court and the Florentine cathedral from 1609 until his death. He founded the Accademia degli Elevati in 1607, an organization devoted to music and populated by composers, instrumentalists, singers, and literati. His best known work was a setting of Rinuccini's *Dafne*, first produced in Mantua during the 1608 Carnival. But he composed a wide variety of music, including a collection of *Musiche a una, dua, e tre voce*, published in Venice in 1615.[8] The volume contains music for a complete *balletto*, settings of sonnets by Petrarch and Bembo, spiritual pieces, and strophic songs. A large portion of the pieces are for two or three sopranos, and clearly demonstrate a dependence upon Luzzaschi's florid style.

Giovanni Battista da Gagliano(1594-1651) also spent his life in Florence as a composer and teacher. He supplied music for several churches, fraternities, and academies, primarily for special festivities. His *Varie musice*(Venice, 1623) also includes pieces for *virtuose* in the north Italian style. The

facsimile example (pp. 70-72) of the fifth
piece in that collection, "Ninfe prole del
Ciel", provides an interesting example of the
north Italian style. The two soprano parts
cover the same tessitura and share equally in
the ornamentation, supported by a figured
bass. The voice parts begin in unison with
fairly substantial *passaggi* lasting through
the triple time section. The return of
quarter time marks the beginning of imitative
phrases, followed by more complicated *passaggi* on the second page of the piece. Simpler,
imitative sections on verses such as "mentre
del mio dolore" [during my sorrow] alternate
with more complex ornamentation until the
piece concludes on a long, difficult embellishment of "Quella belta superba" [this excellent beauty]. The through-composed text
and music are the standard length for this
repertory; the poem, invoking the beauty and
sorrow of a mythical woman, is also typical
of *concerto* material, with its madrigalesque
quality. The music appears in score, rather
than in partbooks, as was common with north
Italian publications. As Luzzaschi perhaps
discovered, it was easier for the women to
practise with all the vocal parts before
them, rather than just their own.

Women's ensemble music composed in the north Italian style was sometimes used for, or influenced by, popular theatrical entertainments. Florence, in particular, hosted a wide variety of musical and dramatic events. Most of the earliest operas were produced there, or involved Florentine composers such Marco da Gagliano, Jacopo Peri, Giulio Caccini, or Emilio de'Cavalieri. The court enjoyed entertainments, especially the *mascherata* and *balletto*; these events featured dancing by both guests and professional dancers, interspersed with dramatic scenes and singing. The court *virtuose* performed at such occasions, just as the Ferrarese *concerto* had provided public entertainment for festive programs.[10]

Both performers and composers provided music for these *intermezzi*. For example, *La mascherata di ninfe di Senna*, performed February 14, 1611, included music by Peri, Marco da Gagliano, Francesca and Settimia Caccini, and Vittoria Archilei.[11] While music sung at such gatherings lacked the intimate setting of a chamber performance, it was stylistically similar.

Furthermore, early operas and *balletti*

were influenced by the popularity of the
women's ensemble. The Florentine composer
Severo Bonini (1582 - 1663) published an
opera, *Lamento d'Ariana*, in 1613. Unlike
most operas, however, this one is listed in
Il Nuovo Vogel because it is actually a collection of pieces for one, two, and three
voices. There are several "choruses" for two
sopranos which are identical in style to virtuoso ensemble music, and Bonini dedicated
the work to the *virtuosi* -- men and women
-- of Florence. In 1623, Francesca Caccini's
opera *La Liberazione di Ruggiero* was performed in Florence. It later became the
first Italian opera to be given outside Italy, when it was performed in Warsaw in 1682.
La Liberazione is also in *Il Nuovo Vogel*, and
contains numerous duets and trios for
sopranos. A chorus of one, two, and three
damigelle [damsels] comment on the action
throughout the work.

Francesca Caccini, a representative of
the Florentine school, was one of the most
significant female composers and performers
of her time. That she is accorded a place in
most 20th-century musical anthologies attests
to her renown, for few other women of the
period have attracted scholarly attention.

While she may have gained access to musical circles of her time through her father, it is evident from descriptions by her contemporaries, and from her surviving compositions, that her musical skills were extraordinary.

The facsimile example (pp. 4-6) of a solo madrigal, "Pieta mercede aita", from her *Primo Libro*(1618), is one of many fine pieces in that collection. The use of phrase markings throughout the piece and the marking for "tri" over notes to be ornamented with the *trillo* are unusual for published scores of the time. Similarly in measure 4, Caccini added a slur between the 'g-sharp' and 'a', an attention to detail that is seldom found in printed scores of that period. While the music has some qualities of ornamented recitative typical of Florentine repertory, the piece is called *madrigale*. The ornamentation, with its 16th and 32nd notes is typical of the north Italian style, and the closing *passaggi* of great length and difficulty are also characteristic of the female ensemble material (it was previously seen in the Gagliano piece).

Florentine academies were often at the

center of new musical developments. While
they usually flourished only briefly, these
groups encouraged performers and composers to
experiment with new methods of singing. A
significant idea, which emerged in part
through Giovanni de'Bardi's *camerata*, was the
use of ornamented recitative. Giulio Caccini
was a foremost member of the *camerata*, which
reached its zenith between 1577 and 1582, and
he was especially involved with this musical
"reform".[12] His collections of *Nuove musiche*,
published in 1601 and 1614, included several
pieces for male voice based on ornamented
recitative. Interestingly, though, Caccini
received the advice from Bardi that he should
use the ladies of Ferrara as an example when
designing his embellishments. Bardi recom-
mended that each line of text should be ex-
pressed properly, and not split into seg-
ments. *Passaggi* should come only on long
syllables:

> The ladies of Ferrara,
> whom Bardi has heard sing
> at least 330 madrigals by
> heart without ever spoil-
> ing a syllable, should be
> his models. 13

Caccini evidently took this advice to heart.
Since he was instrumental in training the

Florentine *virtuose*, and had some impact at least on Francesca's output, it is not surprising that the north Italian style retained many features of Luzzaschi's music for women.

Although Giulio Caccini's embellished recitative was most often associated with opera and monody, some collections in that style were published for one, two and three women. Pietro Benedetti (1585 - 1649), a member of Marco da Gagliano's Accademia degli Elevati, lived in Florence and was apparently a musical dilettante rather than professional composer. His *Musiche a una, et due voci* (Florence, 1617) contains seven pieces for two sopranos which use ornamented recitative. Short, dotted notes are followed by long note values and then by *passaggi* that are well-spaced and similar to those in Luzzaschi's madrigals. The example on the following page is a setting of the well-known madrigal text "Era l'anima mia".

Venice boasted many important publishing houses and several collections for *virtuose* were printed there, but the city did not sponsor its own female ensemble. Musical life centered almost entirely around the

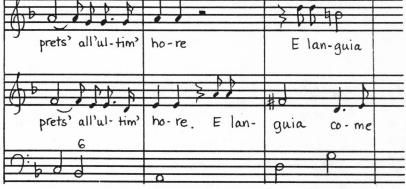

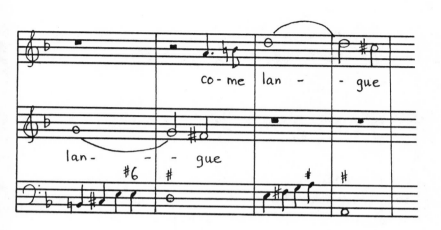

cathedral S. Marco, and even that was in
decline from the 1580s until 1613, when Monteverdi became *maestro di cappella*. Venice
was slow to produce an opera; its first opera
house, S. Cacciano, did not open until 1637.
Before 1640, there was little secular or
dramatic music at court. The Venetian con-
stitution prohibited the celebrations of
royal weddings -- events which prompted
lavish entertainments elsewhere in Italy.
There was never any attempt to organize a
professional *concerto*, which was probably why
Barbara Strozzi's father had to found an
academy to promote her singing.

Nicolò Fontei's collections of *Bizzarrie
poetiche*(Venice, 1635, 1636, and 1639), composed for Barbara Strozzi, are late but significant examples of the north Italian style.
Apart from his efforts, however, Venetian
composers produced little for women's voices.
Composers such as Alessandro Grandi (c.1580 -
1560) and Monteverdi, who did so much to
boost the city's musical reputation, wrote
some duets and trios for male voice. Monteverdi's book VII(1614) includes a few
madrigals for two sopranos, but he was apparently not interested in establishing any
group of professional female singers.

This lack of interest in female ensembles in Venice may have contributed to the later scholarly neglect of this tradition. After 1640, Venice was regarded as a significant center for early Baroque music. Particularly Monteverdi's reputation helped to earn that city a prominent place in history. Had he, or other Venetian composers produced works for specific *virtuose* in Venice, the fame of such ensembles would have been insured. But Venetians were more concerned with instrumental music and opera. As that city became more famous throughout Europe for its great operatic productions, the mystique and charm of the private female ensemble diminished, and finally gave way to the public-oriented spectacle.

NOTES

1. Giustiniani, *Discorso*, p. 70.

2. Rorke, "The Sacred Madrigals of Paolo Quagliati and Antonio Cifra". Prof. Rorke's study gives a history of the sacred madrigal and its relation to the reforms of the Council of Trent.

3. Rorke, "The Sacred Madrigals of Paolo Quagliati and Antonio Cifra", p. 28

4. Newcomb, *The Madrigal at Ferrara*, I:74.

5. Willi Apel, *A History of Keyboard Music to 1700*, trans. and rev. by Hans Tischler. (Bloomington: Indiana University Press, 1972), p. 437.

6. Richard Hudson, "Ruggiero" in *The New Grove Dictionary of Music and Musicians*. XVI:324

7. This source is found in the Newberry Library under "Case VM 1549 V83m".

8. Marco da Gagliano's *Musiche* has been published in a modern edition. Putnam Aldrich, ed., *Marco da Gagliano, Musiche*. Series of Early Music vols. 2, 5. (Bryn Mawr, Pa.: Theodore Presser, 1969-72).

9. An original edition of the collection is found in the Newberry Library of Chicago, apart from the large Roman anthology, under "Case 1549 G13v".

10. Newcomb's research discovered that the *balletto delle donne* was almost as popular in Ferrara as the *concerto*.

11. Raney, "Francesca Caccini", p. 94.

12. Claude V. Palisca, "The 'Camerata fiorentina': a reappraisal", *Studi Musicali*, 1(1972), pp. 203-236.

13. Palisca, "The 'Camerata fiorentina'", p. 216.

Albini, Filippo. *Musicali concenti* ... *A una,
    due, et quattro voci*. Milan, 1623.

> *Il Secondo Libro dei Musicali
>   Concerti ... ad una, e
>   due voci*. Rome, 1626.

The first collection contains virtuosic music
for special court festivities including the
opening solo, "La Notte", in honor of Duke
Carlo Emanuelle's birthday, spiritual works,
and several simpler *arie*. Besides soprano
solos, Albini provides duets for both two
sopranos and soprano and tenor. The dedications to three pieces, two highly virtuosic,
specifically mention a female performer at
the court, Isabella Colleata. Colleata, who
first performed the highly virtuosic "La
Notte", is described in the collection as a
Cantatrice Virtuossissima [sic] *e musica*.
Two other women, Margherita Maroni and
Isabella Pongini, are mentioned as dedicatees
for individual *arie spirituale*, though it is
unclear whether they were true performers or
merely important members of the court. Male
musicians, or *musico*, Prosperio Marisio and
Luiggi Ravetto are also mentioned, but
without further references to their abilities
or specific court activities.

Book II, written after Albini moved to Rome,
contains fifteen solos and only three duets.
The music is quite similar to book I, and Albini again set spiritual verses as well as
texts which reflect special activities and
celebrations within his employer's court.

Albini (c.1580 - c.1626) replaced Sigismondo d'India as the chief composer of the Savoy court in Turin, and he later worked for the Duke of Savoy's son, Cardinal Maurizio, in Rome. His collections obviously reflect the musical tastes of the Savoy court.

Anerio, Giovanni Francesco. *Selva armonica. Dove si contengono Motetti, Madrigali, Canzonette, Dialoghi, Arie a una, doi, tre, et quattro voci.* Rome, 1617.

> *La Bella Clori armonica. Arie, Canzonetti, e Madrigali, a una due et tre voce.* Rome, 1619.

Selva Armonica, set entirely to sacred Italian and Latin texts, combines works in both virtuosic and simple styles. The majority of works are for solo, some suitable for soprano or tenor performance according to the *tavola*, and one work is for *basso* solo. Of the three-voice works, one is a Latin "Litanie" to the Virgin Mary.

La Bella Clori contains again a mixture of simpler and more virtuosic repertory and features works in the Roman three-voice texture. In these three-voice works, the bass voice has an equal share in the virtuosic writing. Many of the works are quite long with several *parti* in different meters.

G. F. Anerio was an ordained priest and spent most of his life in Rome, though later he became *maestro di capella* to King Sigismund III of Poland.

Banchieri, Adriano. *Il   Virtuoso   Ritrovo*
    Academico del   Dissonante, publicamente
    praticato con variati Concerti   musicali
    a 1. 2. 3. 4. 5. voci o stromenti,
    nell'Academia de Filomusi. Venice, 1626.

The collection contains madrigals for one and
two sopranos in the north Italian style, with
emphasis on ornamented recitative. There is
also a large cycle for solo tenor composed
over the *ruggiero* bass, and instrumental
pieces using the *gran duca* and *romanesca* basses. All pieces employ a wide tessitura,
numerous difficult vocal leaps, and substantial ornamentation.

Banchieri(1568-1634) was a Benedictine monk
and lived in Bologna. This volume was dedicated to the Academia de Filomusi, which
Banchieri helped to found in   1615. (It was
first called the Accademia dei Floridi.) The
music was probably written with specific performers of the academy in mind.

Bellante, Dionisio. *Concerti academici a una,*
    due,   tre,   quattro, cinque, et sei
    voci. Venice, 1629.

Of the thirty-two pieces, seventeen are for
two sopranos and five are for three voices.
A large cycle of nine *parti*, "Quand'i mi vol-
go", for two sopranos and composed over the
romanesca bass, is the highlight of the collection. Pieces for more than three voices
include instrumental parts, so there are

never more than three singers involved. The
Roman style is favored, with long, elaborate
ornamentation of nearly every phrase.

Bellante (? - 1642) lived in Verona. The
title pages of his published works suggest
that he was an amateur composer, but connected with an academy whose professional
concern was solely music.

Benedetti, Pietro. *Musiche ... a una, e dua
     voci   con   alcune   spirituali   nel
     fine.* Florence, 1617.

The collection includes twenty solo pieces
for tenor or soprano and seven pieces for two
sopranos. While the solo pieces are often
strophic, the works for two sopranos are virtuosic, in the north Italian style with emphasis on ornamented recitative. Range is
not extreme, but dissonance is often used between voices.

Benedetti (1585 - c.1649) spent most of his
life in Florence. In 1608 he travelled to
Mantua to help with musical arrangements for
Francesco Gonzaga's wedding and met their
virtuose. A musical dilettante, he was affiliated with the Florentine Accademia degli
Elevati, for which his works were composed.

Bernardi, Stefano. *Concerti academici con
     varie sorte di Sinfonie.* Venice, 1615.

     *Madrigaletti a due et a tre
     voci.* Venice, 1621.

*Il Primo Libro de' Madrigali a
tre voci*. Venice, 1621.

The *Concerti academici* collection includes
ten pieces for one and two women, with an
especially noteworthy cycle of five *parti* on
a Petrarch text, "Lasso, ch'io ardo", for two
sopranos. There are also several *sinfonie*
for instruments. The vocal pieces are usually preceded by a brief instrumental *ritornello* and are in the north Italian style. There
is no *basso continuo* part provided.

The *Madrigaletti* follow a similar pattern,
with pieces for two sopranos, tenor and alto,
and soprano and alto. The instrumental
pieces call for bassoon, cornetti, chitar-
rone, trombone, and violin.

Il primo Libro de' Madrigali is entirely for
three voices, primarily two sopranos and
alto, and features the north Italian style.

Bernardi (1585 - 1636) was trained as a
singer in Verona, then spent some years in
Rome where he was *maestro di cappella* at the
Madonna dei Monti. In 1611, he returned to
Verona to assume leadership at the Verona
cathedral and was associated with the Accademia Filarmonica, for which these works
were evidently composed. In 1622, he moved
to Salzburg as a musician for Archduke Carl
Joseph and remained there until his death.

Biandra', Giovan Pietro. *Il Primo Libro de
      Madrigaletti a una doi e tre voci*. Ven-
      ice, 1626.

This sacred collection, dedicated to the Accademia degli Spennati Musici in Faenza, contains a variety of works for all voice ranges. Though entitled *Madrigaletti*, the sub-
title at the bottom of each page, *Madr. e
Arie Spirituali*, belies the inclusion of both
simple, strophic pieces, which are clearly
segregated at the end of the publication, and
sacred-texted works. The solos in all voice
ranges, and duets for a variety of voice combinations, indicate that the publication may
have been a practical one featuring music for
all the soloists and performers associated
with the Accademia.

Biandra' (fl.1610 - 1630) called himself
Romano maestro and may have worked in Rome
before becoming *maestro di cappella* of the
cathedral in Faenza. He later became *maestro
di cappella* for the Accademia degli Spennati,
to whom he dedicated a second publication as
well. Biandra' also wrote sacred music for
two to four voices.

Bizzarro Accademico Capriccioso. *Il Secondo
    Libro de Trastulli estivi concertati a
    due, tre, et quattro voci*. Venice, 1621.

This composer is only known by the name "Bizzarro", which he assumed in the Accademico
Capriccioso. His surviving works were all
published during the 1620s and dedicated to
the virtuoso performers of his academy. This
collection also refers to performers at other
Italian academies: The Intronati in Siena,
the Pellegrini in Florence, the Olimpici in
Vicenza, and the Filarmonici in Verona. The
pieces are mainly for two and three voices,
with five for two sopranos, and one for two

altos. There is some emphasis on ornamented recitative, though the collection is an excellent example of north Italian style with its imitative ornamentation and contrasting textures. The voices ranges overlap and are not extreme.

Bonini, Severo. *Affetti spirituali a dua voci parte in istile di Firenze o recitativo per modo di Dialogo, e parte in istile misto*. Venice, 1615.

This collection, almost entirely for two sopranos, features sacred madrigals and motets with Latin texts. Bonini worked in the monastery at Valombrosa and was organist at S. Mercuriale at Forle (both near Florence), and the pieces undoubtedly were composed for talented nuns affiliated with those institutions. In the north Italian style, there are often only a few ornamented passages per piece; while these are difficult and extend into the upper range, the remainder of the music is imitative and lyrical.

Bonini (1582 - 1663), a Benedictine monk, worked in various parishes near Florence. He was a friend and enthusiastic supporter of Giulio Caccini, and the title page of this volume suggests his interest in ornamented recitative. While his compositions show a mixture of styles, recitative is not usually favored; there is more emphasis on contrasting, slow-moving passages with *passaggi*.

Borboni, Nicolo. *Musicali concenti a una, e
    due voci*. Rome, 1618.

This Roman collection primarily contains
works for the solo voice and settings of both
sacred and secular texts. The publication
opens with six sectional works, designated as
sonetti, followed by five *madrigali*, five
arie (including two on the *romanesca* bass),
and seven strophic *canzonetti*. The most virtuosic works, the *sonetti* and *madrigali*, are
highly ornamented with long and inventive
passaggi. The sign for the *trillo* ornament
appears frequently in the solo works. The
three works for two sopranos include a can-
zonetta, a sectional work on the *romanesca*
bass, and a virtuosic madrigal. Some of the
works feature instrumental *ritornelli*.

Borboni (fl.1614 - 1641) appears to have
spent most of his life in Rome as an organ
builder, music engraver, and later organist
at S. Giovanni in Laterano. He engraved his
own music as well as some later publications
by Frescobaldi.

Brunetti, Domenico. *L'Euterpe ... opera
    musicale di Madrigali, Canzonette, Arie,
    Stanze, e Scherzi diversi, in Dialoghi,
    e Echo, a una, due, tre et quattro voci,
    da cantarsi in Theorba, Arpicordo, et
    altri stromenti*. Venice, 1606.

This early publication contains works mainly
for solo (a total of sixteen) and in a
variety of styles, as stated in the title.
The solo works, as well as the four duets,
demonstrate an interest in florid writing.
Several of the solos are in the tenor and

bass clefs, and two of the duets combine male and female voice ranges as well.

Brunetti (c.1580 - 1646) was born in Bologna and served as organist and *maestro di cappella* at the Bolognese cathedral. Some of his later sacred works, Latin-texted solos, duets, and trios, may reflect an adaptation of virtuosic technique to the sacred repertory.

Caccini, Francesca. *Il Primo Libro delle Musiche a una, e due voci*. Florence, 1618.

This collection was published when Caccini was thirty years old and at the zenith of her singing career. All but four of the thirty-six pieces are for solo and were originally composed for her own use. The table of contents advertises madrigals, canzonettas, sonnet settings, strophic variations, and some sacred pieces on Latin texts, suggesting that she tried to display her vocal and compositional skills in a variety of ways. There are only a few canzonettas and strophic variations, while the rest of the collection employs both the Roman and north Italian styles. Scholars have suggested that Francesca was influenced by her father's interest in ornamented recitative, but these pieces show only occasional use of that technique. There are several arias over the *romanesca* bass, and these pieces are appropriately in the Roman tradition with extensive ornamentation. Other pieces demonstrate the north Italian style, with alternating slow and embellished passages; these often include an elaborate *basso continuo* part. Caccini was

one of the few composers to indicate ornaments, such as the *trillo*, slurs, and other
phrase groupings. The pieces for two voices
are for soprano and bass. For further
biography on Francesca Caccini, see the appendix. Some pieces from Caccini's *Primo
Libro* are transcribed in Carolyn Raney,
"Francesca Caccini, Musician to the Medici"
(Ph.D. dissertation, New York University,
1971).

Calestani, Vicenzo. *Madrigali et Arie per
    sonare et cantare nel Chitarrone Leuto o
    Clavicembalo, a una, e due voci*. Venice,
    1617.

Only two works from this predominately solo
collection are available in modern edition. (Knud Jeppesen, ed. *La Flora*. Copen-
hagen, 1949, volumes 1, 3.) We were unable
to obtain a microfilm copy of the entire collection. It is still a publication worth
noting because of its dedication to Isabella
Malespini Mastiani, a member of a leading
family in Pisa. Calestani(1589-c.1617)
taught music to Isabella and claimed, in the
dedication to this publication, that he
served as her accompanist in performance.
Whether Isabella was a true professional *virtuosa* or a talented amateur is unknown. Certainly this publication represents the spread
of music for women to Pisa.

Campana, Francesca. *Arie a una, due, e tre
    voci*. Rome, 1629.

As the title indicates, the majority of the

works in this collection are in a simple,
strophic style. The opening solos, the two
duets for two *canti*, and the two works in the
three-voice Roman texture, show more virtuosic features. In the three-voice works,
the upper two voices are more florid, and no
separate *basso continuo* part is given, but
must be derived from the bass line.

Campana (? - 1665) was a Roman singer and
spinet player as well as a composer, and she
evidently wrote music for her own use. Many
virtuose composed for their own use, but most
of their output circulated in manuscript and
is now lost. Campana was fortunate to have
had the opportunity to publish her works.

Capece, Alessandro. *Il Secondo Libro de
    Madrigali, et Arie a una, due, et tre
    voci*. Rome, 1625.

This collection, which appears in the Newberry Library volume (see discussion on pages
67-68), again demonstrates the stylistic differences between the late 16th-century virtuosic madrigal and the simpler *arie* of the
early 17th-century. The format follows Luzzaschi's with seven solos (all for soprano),
five duets, and ten trios. All the trios are
in the three-voice Roman texture, and several
of the duets use male voices as well. The
opening solo is the most virtuosic piece in
the collection.

Capece (fl.1610 - 1636) spent most of his
life in the service of cathedrals in various
Italian cities, including Ferrara, Sulmona,
Naples and Tivoli. He wrote primarily sacred
music, much of which is lost. Besides this

collection, his *opera seconda*, he published
two books of madrigals for four and five
voices.

Ceresini, Giovanni. *Madrigali concertati a
       due, tre, e quattro voci con il Basso
       continuo*. Venice, 1627.

This Venetian publication contains
predominately duets for a variety of voice
combinations, with the *canto* voice favored
overall. The pieces are in the north Italian
style, featuring a great deal of imitation.

Ceresini (1584 - c.1659) worked in Ferrara
from 1612 on as *maestro di cappella* for the
Accademia delle Morte, a charitable organization. He later worked at the Ferrarese
cathedral. This collection, published fifteen years after his arrival in Ferrara,
probably represents music written for, and
performed by, various members of Ceresini's
Accademia.

Cesana, Bertolomeo. *Musiche a una doi et tre
       voci per cantare et sonare con Chitaroni
       overo con altri istromenti di cor-
       po*. Venice, 1613.

The collection of fourteen pieces was
designed to imitate Luzzaschi's *Madrigali* of
1601, with pieces for one, followed by two,
and then for three voices. The volume was
printed in score format, rather than in
partbooks, again like Luzzaschi's book, and

the pieces are good examples of the north
Italian style. Those for one and two voices
are for soprano, while the three-part works
are for a variety of voice ranges. While the
title specifies chitarone accompaniment, the
basso continuo part can be played by any instrument.

Cesana (c.1580 - 1623), actually Bertolomeo
Mutis, Count of Cesana, was chaplain and
singer at the court of Archduke Ferdinand at
Graz, and later in Vienna. This volume was
one of the first collections for singing
ladies to be published by a composer working
in Austria.

Cifra, Antonio. *Scherzi sacri   ... A una, a
    due, a tre, a quattro voci. Libro
    Primo.* Rome, 1616.

    *Scherzi sacri   ... a una, a
        due, a tre, a quattro
        voci. Libro Secondo.*
        Rome, 1618.

    *Li Diversi Scherzi ... a una,
        a due, et tre voci.* Rome,
        1613.

    *Li Diversi Scherzi ... a una,
        a due, et tre voci. Libro
        Secondo.* Rome, 1613.

    *Scherzi et Arie a una, due,
        tre, et quattro voci per
        cantar nel Clavicembalo,
        Chitarrone, o altro simi-
        le istromento.* Venice,
        1614.

> *Li Diversi Scherzi ... a una,
> a due, a tre, et quattro
> voci. Libro Quarto.* Rome,
> 1615.

> *Li Diversi Scherzi ... A una,
> a due, a tre, et quattro
> voci. Libro Quinto.* Rome,
> 1617.

> *Libro Sesto di Scherzi ... a
> una, due, tre, e quattro
> voci.* [Rome], 1619.

The two sacred collections, published while
Cifra was still *maestro di cappella* at Santa
Casa di Loreto, contain virtuosic solos for
soprano, tenor, and baritone, duets for two
sopranos over bass patterns, and simpler
three and four-voice works. Cifra may have
composed these works for specific occasions
at Santa Casa, and the florid solos for tenor
and baritone indicate the presence of male
virtuosi.

The first two collections of *Diversi Scherzi*
contain more duets and trios than solos. The
solos are florid works written over active
basso continuo lines. Most of the duets are
on bass patterns featuring at times high tessitura, imitation, running passages in
thirds, and other ornamentation.

The *Scherzi et Arie* (actually book III of
Diversi Scherzi) and book IV of *Diversi
Scherzi* have an equal number of solos and
duets. The solos are still virtuosic, though
occasionally more in the style of ornamented
recitative with *passaggi* reserved for caden-
tial points. In these two collections all
duets are written on bass patterns. *Scherzi*

et Arie contains two interesting four-voice works, set for SATB and *basso continuo*. Both pieces, in four *parti*, have elaborately orna- mented lines in all four voices, which is uncharacteristic of Cifra's usual polyphonic madrigal style. Perhaps these works were meant for a specific female and male ensemble either in Rome, Loreto, or even in Venice, where the collection was published.

Cifra's last two collections show a shift to solo repertory with the number of solo works out-numbering the duets, and the application of the bass pattern technique to the solo voice. Book V alludes to a group of *virtuose* in the employ of Duchess Cornelia Caetana di Cesarini, though nothing more specific is known. Book VI was written in Florence and is dedicated to Antonio de Medici. The solo works, some set to bass patterns, are the most virtuosic examples in Cifra's output with consistent use of ornamentation throughout. This change in Cifra's style for his last collection may demonstrate his wish to impress the Medici court, or show the in- fluence of a special singer in their employ. For more information on Cifra, see the dis- cussion on pages 63-66.

Crivellati, Domenico. *Cantate diverse a una, due, e tre voci, con l'intavolatura per la Chitarra spagnola in quelle più ap- proposito.*   Rome, 1628.

The collection follows Luzzaschi's format for one, two, and then three voices, but the majority of works are for soprano solo. There are five pieces for two, and two pieces

104   Annotated Bibliography

for three voices. The vocal parts are in the
north Italian style, with emphasis on ornamented recitative. But some of the pieces
also employ an instrumental *ritornello* over
the *ruggiero* bass. The singer or singers are
instructed to stop at certain points so the
interlude can be played; then the vocalists
resume with their parts.

Little is known about Crivellati (fl.1628).
This is his only publication, and the title
page notes that he lived in Viterbo, an ecclesiastical province north of Rome.

d'India, Sigismondo. *Le Musiche ... da cantar
      solo nel Clavicordo Chitarone Arpa dop-
      pia et altri istromenti.* Milan, 1609.

      Le Musiche a due voci. Venice,
         1615.

      *Le Musiche ... Libro Terzo a
         una e due voci.* Milan,
         1618.

      *Le Musiche ... a una et due
         voci da cantarasi nel
         Chitarrone Clavicembalo,
         Arpa doppia et altri
         stromenti da corpo. Libro
         Quarto.* Venice, 1621.

      *Le Musiche ... da cantarsi nel
         Chitarrone, Clavicembalo
         Arpa doppia, et altri
         stromenti da corpo. Libro
         Quinto.* Venice, 1623.

Sigismondo d'India is most known for his
monodic compositions which account for the
majority of his works in the collections of
1609, 1618, 1621, and 1623. His solo compositions encompass a wide variety of techniques and styles including simple settings of
short texts, works composed over bass patterns, expressive use of chromaticism, and
richly ornamented settings of longer, more
well-known madrigal texts. The dedication to
the large 1609 collection states that the
noted *virtuosa*, Vittoria Archilei, as well as
other famous soloists, had performed
d'India's compositions. The 1609 collection
is available in a modern edition by Federico
Mompellio.

The duets which comprise the 1615 publication, as well as the handful appearing in the
other four collections, are for two sopranos
or two tenors and *basso continuo* and feature
contrasting sections of ornamented imitation
and homophony. D'India made use of the
repeating bass pattern technique for his
duets as well, most often favoring the *ruggiero* bass.

Sigismondo d'India (c.1582 - c.1669), of
Sicilian birth, was employed at the court of
Savoy in Turin from 1611-1623. The Savoy
Duke, Carlo Emanuelle, was a patron of the
arts, and d'India's four later collections no
doubt reflect the musical interests and
tastes of the court. Filippo Albini, who
replaced d'India as court composer, made
reference in his publication of 1623 to court
virtuosi, in particular the soprano Isabella
Colleata, and probably d'India's works were
written for specific court performers as
well. After his tenure at Turin, d'India
worked in other Italian cities including
Rome, Mantua, and Modena. Prof. Glenn Wat-

kins, of the University of Michigan, is
presently editing the complete works of
d'India as part of the *Musiche rinascimenti
siciliane* series.

Donati, Ignazio. *Le Fanfalughe a due, tre,
   quattro, et cinque voci.* Venice, 1630.

Duets set for a variety of vocal combinations
make up most of this collection. As with
other collections of this nature, the *canto*
voice is used most often, and all four three-
voice works combine two *canti* and bass.

Donati (c.1575 - 1638) composed mainly sacred
works, including motets for a small number of
voices. His sacred publication *Concerti Ec-
clesiastici*(1618) contains works for three
sopranos. He held a variety of church posts
throughout Italy, including positions in Urbino, Pesaro, Fano, Ferrara, Novara, Lodi,
and Milan.

Fontei, Nicolò. *Bizzarrie poetiche ... a
   1.2.3. voci.* Venice, 1635.

      *Bizzarrie poetiche ... Libro
         Secondo. A una, doi, e
         tre voci.* Venice, 1636.

      *Delle Bizzarrie Poetiche a
         1. 2. 3. voci. Libro Ter-
         zo.* Venice, 1639.

These collections were composed for the
Venetian singer Barbara Strozzi. The dedica-

tion to the first book states that the music
was intended for various meetings of Fontei's
academy, and were written

> primarily for the gentle
> *virtuosissima donzelle*,
> Signora Barbara. She
> gave me occasion to com-
> pose them, and gives your
> Honor [Paolo Vidmano] the
> occasion to hear them
> performed.

The dedication to the second book notes that

> these harmonious works,
> called Bizzarrie Poeti-
> che, animated largely by
> the texts of Giulio
> Strozzi, are for the use
> of his *virtuosissima can-
> tatrice*.

Book I is largely for solo voice, with two
pieces for two women, and one for three
voices. Book II includes several solos, but
also an elaborate series of dialogues for the
poetic characters, Tirsi and Chloris. The
basso continuo part frequently includes
scalar passages, sometimes with chord indica-
tions for guitar and sometimes with instrumental *ritornelli*. While the solo works
in both collections are extremely difficult,
there is still a north Italian emphasis on
shifting textures and juxtaposed tempi; Fontei even used the affect marking *adagio*
(quite rare for the time) to set off the
slow-moving, unadorned passages. The works
for two and three voices all fall into the
north Italian style.

Book III, which makes no mention of Barbara

Strozzi, is somewhat different from the earlier collections. It is published in score
format, instead of partbooks, and includes a
separate volume for the *basso continuo*. The
basso continuo partbook contains at the back
eighteen *pianto madrigali*, for solo soprano
and virtuoso *basso continuo*, which are not
listed in the table of contents for the main
collection. These must have been composed
for someone of Strozzi's skills, and are Fontei's most difficult pieces. The main collection, as described in the table of contents, includes several strophic, but ornamented works, with nine pieces for two and
three voices.

Fontei (? - c.1647) was born near Pesaro and
spent most of his life in Venice, where he
was associated with the Strozzi family. He
served as organist at S. Maria de Crociccheri
in Venice and may have become a priest around
1639. He was also affiliated with the Accademia degli Unisoni, founded by Giulio
Strozzi for his daughter's performances.

Frescobaldi, Girolamo. *Primo Libro d'Arie
     musicali per cantarsi nel Gravicembalo,
     e Tiorba. A una, a dua, e a tre
     voci*. Florence, 1630.

     *Secondo Libro d'Arie musicali
          per cantarsi nel
          Gravicembalo, e Tiorba. A
          una, a due, e a tre
          voci*. Florence, 1630.

Both collections, published in Florence, display a variety of compositional styles: works
on spiritual texts, solos in *stile*

recitativo, *arie*, simple imitative two-voice
canzoni, and works on bass patterns. Frescobaldi supplied music for male and female
voices, and most of the duets are for *canto*
and tenor. In general, the collections show
a departure from purely virtuosic writing and
a move toward the simple aria as the titles
suggest.

Frescobaldi was raised in Ferrara and studied
with Luzzaschi, thus making him well aware of
the tradition of the *virtuosa*. He spent his
musical life in and out of Rome, as organist
at St. Peter's cathedral and in the employ of
Cardinal Aldobrandini. He also worked for
the Medici family as court organist during
the early 1630s when these two collections
were published. Enzo Bentivoglio, a patron
of Frescobaldi and whose mother had been a
singer of some reputation, attempted to ar-
range a marriage between Frescobaldi and one
of the singing Caccini daughters in order to
foster Bentivoglio's group of singing ladies
in Rome. The marriage did not come about,
and one can only speculate what repertory
such a union could have produced. These two
collections appear in a modern edition: Helga
Spohr, ed. *Arie Musicali* (Mainz: Schott,
1960).

Gagliano, Giovanni Battista da. *Varie musiche
... Libro Primo*. Venice, 1623.

The collection includes a variety of music
for both tenor and soprano and is haphazardly
organized. There are several solo pieces for
virtuoso soprano, but there are also simpler
canzonettas for the amateur performer.
Gagliano specified in the dedication that the

music was designed "not only for the *vir-tuosa*, but for the noble family", presumably the family for whom he worked. The pieces for *virtuose* are interesting examples of the north Italian style, as the piece for two sopranos, "Ninfe, prole del Ciel" demonstrates (see facsimile example pages 70-72).

Giovanni Battista (1594 - 1651), younger brother of Marco da Gagliano, spent his life in Florence where he sang and provided music for numerous institutions. He composed an oratorio, "Il martiro di S. Agata", now lost, with Francesca Caccini, and some of the pieces in his *Varie Musiche* were probably intended for her.

Gagliano, Marco da. *Musiche a una dua e tre voci*. Venice, 1615.

This volume contains a variety of music composed for Florentine court functions. There is a complete *balletto*, "Ballo di donne turche", for three sopranos and tenor, settings of sonnets by Petrarch and Bembo, spiritual madrigals, and a few strophic songs. Most of the pieces are for two sopranos. There are also solo soprano works, pieces for two sopranos plus tenor or bass, and instrumental works. Most pieces are in the north Italian style; in those for two or three sopranos and bass or tenor, the male voice functions as a harmonic bass, and does not share in the ornamentation.

Marco Zenobi, known as Marco da Gagliano, was born in Florence in 1582, and died there in 1643. As *maestro di cappella* for nearly

thirty-five years at the Medici court and
S. Maria del Fiore, he was an important musical figure in that city. He founded the
Florentine Accademia degli Elevati in 1607,
composed an opera "Daphne"(1608), and also
provided five-voice madrigals for the *virtuosi* of Florence. His *Sacrum Can-
tionum*(1622-1623) for one to six voices, composed for private devotions of the Medici
family, also includes some virtuosic music
for sopranos. This collection appears in a
modern edition: Putnam Aldrich, ed. *Marco da
Gagliano, Musiche*, Series of Early Music,
vols. 2,5 (Bryn Mawr, Pa.: Theodore
Presser, 1969-72).

Giamberti, Giuseppe. *Poesie diverse ... a una
    due e tre voci per cantar nel Cimbalo et
    alcune con l'alfabeto per la Chitarra
    spagnola.* Rome, 1623.

Solo repertory for male and female voice
dominates this collection found in the Newberry Library volume. Virtuosic solos for
soprano, tenor, bass, and baritone appear, as
well as works in a simpler style.

Giamberti (c.1600 - c.1622) was a student of
Giovanni Nanino and Paolo Agostini, and one
work by each composer appears in this collection. Giamberti held church positions
primarily in Rome.

Guazzi, Eleuterio. *Spirituosi affetti a una e
    due voci. Madrigali e Romanesca.* Venice,

1622.

This book consists entirely of secular works,
despite the title, and all pieces are for one
and two sopranos. There are a few strophic
canzonettas for solo soprano at the beginning
of the volume, but the other works are extremely virtuosic, in the Roman style but
without male voice. Several pieces, including the cycle of four texts from Guarini's
"Cosi m'ha fatt'amor", use the *romanesca*
bass. The composer employed written-out
trilli among the ornamentation.

Guazzi (1597 - c.1622), born in Parma, was a
singer at the court chapel of that city until
1621. He apparently received a post in Venice, but died shortly after arriving. This
collection, published posthumously, is his
only known work.

Kapsberger, Johannes Hieronymus. *Libro Secon-
    do d'Arie a una e più voci*. Rome, 1623.

This is a very ornately printed edition, with
a flower border and the composer's initials
on each page. There are twenty-one pieces,
plus a four-part cycle for solo soprano, and
five pieces for either two sopranos or
soprano and bass. The music is in the Roman
style, covering a wide vocal range, and containing several large leaps between *passaggi*.
The original publication may also include
interesting clues for early Baroque phrasing:
the 8th, 16th, and 32nd notes use barring
rather than individual flags for each pitch
(the latter practice being the usual one for
such publications). The notes are obviously
barred together to achieve various phrase

groupings, and these groupings include from three to ten notes.

Kapsberger (c.1580 - 1651) was a German nobleman, but was born in Venice where he made his home until 1604. He spent the rest of his life in Rome, largely as a professional lutenist. He was a significant composer in the development of a virtuoso style for plucked instruments, characterized by trills, slides, and tremolos. His vocal music employs a similar style, forming an interesting synthesis between vocal and instrumental practices. Kapsberger also published four books of *villanelle* for one to three voices, and a volume for solo soprano.

Luzzaschi, Luzzasco. *Madrigali per cantare, et sonare a uno, e doi, e tre soprani*. Rome, 1601.

Our entire study begins here with Luzzaschi's works for the original Ferrarese *concerto*. The distinctive format of this collection -- the works grouped together by number of voices -- was an aspect copied by later composers of virtuosic repertory. Luzzaschi published three solos, four duets, and five trios, featuring the written-out ornamentation for which the singing ladies were famous. A further aspect of this work is the keyboard accompaniment which is not a figured bass, but rather is written-out for both hands, usually doubling the voice parts.

Luzzaschi (1545 - 1607) studied with the madrigal composer Cipriano de Rore and later became the *maestro di cappella* for the Ferrarese court. He was a keyboard player of

great reputation and made a name for himself
as one of the few people able to play Nicolò
Vicentino's keyboard creation, the *arcicem-
balo*. Luzzaschi was also highly regarded as
a polyphonic madrigal composer, producing
seven books of five-voice madrigals.

Marini, Biagio. *Madrigaletti a una due tre e
    quatro voci, con alcune Vilanele ... con
    il suo Basso Continuo*. Venice, 1635.

The title of this collection and the rather
late publication date indicate the presence
of works in a less virtuosic vein. And the
solos, for all voice ranges, are in a simpler
style, but the ten duets, for a variety of
two-voice combinations, are typical of the
north Italian florid style. The combination
of works for all ranges and Marini's affilia-
tion with the Accademico Occulto, suggest
that this collection was probably assembled
from music performed at the academy by its
members and soloists.

Marini (c.1587 - 1663), best known as an instrumental composer, began his musical career
in Venice as a violinist at S. Marco. His
major appointment was as *Kapellmeister* to the
Wittelsbach court at Neuberg, though during
this time he still retained Italian ties and
later returned to northern Italy. Towards
the end of his life, he also wrote sacred
Latin-texted works for a small number of
voices and *basso continuo*.

Monteverdi, Claudio. *Concerto Settimo Libro*

*de Madrigali   a   1.   2.   3.   4.   et   sei
voci.* Venice, 1619.

*Madrigali et Canzonette a due,
    e tre voci.* Venice, 1651.

Selva Morale   e   Spirituale.
    Venice, 1641.

Most   of   Monteverdi's   later   collections
featuring   works   for   one,   two,   and   three
voices favor the male voice, though the rela-
tively small number of works for sopranos are
lavish examples of the virtuosic style. Book
VII, dedicated to his   employer   Caterina   de
Medici   Gonzaga,   contains five duets for two
sopranos, including one work in four   stanzas
composed   over the *romanesca* bass. The duets
are in the north Italian style, with much imitation of virtuosic writing between   voices.
The one three-voice work for two sopranos and
bass   is   equally difficult in all voices and
the bass achieves a remarkable degree of   in-
dependence from the *basso continuo* line.

Though   much of *Madrigali e Canzonette* is for
male voice, the collection does   contain   one
work for three sopranos. This composition in
four   stanzas   is   very   much in the style of
Luzzaschi.

The *Selva Morale*, as well as volume 16 of the
Malipero modern   edition   containing   miscel-
laneous   sacred   works,   includes some lovely
solos and duets on sacred Latin   texts.   The
"Et   resurrexis"   of *Selva Morale* is for two
sopranos concerted with two violins.

Claudio Monteverdi (1567 - 1643)   is   undoubtedly the most famous composer of the Italian
madrigal.   Though   his   later collections of
polyphonic madrigals feature virtuosic   writ-

ing as well as the use of *basso continuo*, Monteverdi appears to have been less involved with virtuoso performers or specific ensembles than others of his day, except as a composer of early opera. The Mantuan *virtuosa*, Caterina Martinelli, lived with the Monteverdi family for a time, and Monteverdi's wife, Claudia, was herself a singer employed by the Gonzaga court.

Notari, Angelo. *Prime Musiche Nuove ... a una, due, et tre voci*. London, 1613.

The music is composed for a variety of voice combinations, though most pieces are for two sopranos. This volume offers both English and Italian prefaces, in which the composer instructs vocalists on the methods for embellishing in the proper manner. His work was significant for its introduction of ornamented vocal styles into England. The pieces are mainly in the north Italian style, but a few use the *romanesca* bass and are more ornate.

Although Notari (1566 - 1663) was born in Padua and was an early member of the Venetian Accademia degli Sprovisti, he moved to London around 1610. He served the royal family there until his death at the age of ninety-seven.

Olivieri, Giuseppe. *La Pastorella Armilla variamente cantata a una, a due, e tre voci ... per sonare in ogni stromento, l'alfabeto della Chitarra, un Dialogo a*

tre, et una Canzone concertata a cinque.
Rome, 1620.

The *tavola* of this volume again distinguishes
between *madrigali* for one and two voices, and
the simpler and strophic *ariette* for one,
two, and three voices. The majority of works
in the collection are for solo soprano with
the solo madrigals in the style of ornamented
recitative. The entire publication is a pastoral drama of sorts, with the main charac-
ter, or heroine of the story, being the
shepherdess Armilla.

Little is known about Olivieri (? - c.1623)
though the presence of this, one of his two
surviving secular publications, in the Newberry Library source alongside more famous
Roman composers, indicates that he was valued
in his time. His other secular publication,
*La turca armoniosa giovenili ardori a due, e
tre voci*(Rome, 1617) is written entirely for
two tenors and bass, and some works are quite
florid and attest to the Roman interest in
male *virtuosi*. Olivieri held positions in
the court of the Duke of Altemps and as
maestro di cappella at S. Giovanni in
Laterano in Rome.

Orlandi, Camillo. *Arie, a tre, due et voce
sola.* Venice, 1616.

Despite the title, this volume contains some
very virtuosic pieces, referred to as
madrigali in the *tavola*. The solos are in
the style of ornamented recitative, often
with long florid passages, fast moving *basso
continuo* lines, and with the indication of
trillo ornaments. The duets are in the north

Italian style, featuring imitation, ornamented sections, and changes of meter. Orlandi states that the six duets may be performed by two sopranos, or two tenors. The
two three-voice works are dialogues between
mythological characters and are scored for
male and female voices in ornamented recitative.

Orlandi (fl.1616), like Cesana, was one of
many Italian composers who worked outside of
Italy and brought the tradition of the *virtuose* to other parts of the Holy Roman Em-
pire. By the publication date of this work,
his one surviving secular collection, Orlandi
was in the service of Marco Sittico, the
Archbishop of Salzburg.

Quagliati, Paolo. *Affetti amorosi spirituali
      ... dedicati all'ill.ma et molto rev.da
      suor Anna Maria Cesi monaca di S.ta
      Lucia in Selici*. Rome, 1617.

      La Sfera armoniosa.   Rome,
          1623.

The *Affetti spirituali*, on Italian sacred
texts, were written for Sister Anna Maria
Cesi, a nun at the convent of S. Lucia who
was renowned for her vocal performances (see
appendix). Quagliati wrote in the dedication:

                I thought to mark them
                with the name of your
                most Illustrious Lady-
                ship, in order to make
                clear to the world my
                bondage and particular

> regard of you, and also
> because the material and
> the name of the work con-
> form very well with the
> affection of Your Most
> Illustrious   Ladyship
> toward the Celestial
> Lord. And I add that the
> same compositions were
> first cherished and
> favored by you, when
> sometimes you took
> pleasure in singing and
> embellishing them with
> your artful manners and
> most exquisite voice.

The collection includes twenty-two pieces for
three voices. Most works are in the Roman
style, though without bass patterns; there
are also some simpler *villanelle*.

La Sfera armoniosa was composed for the wedding of Nicolo Ludovisi and Isabella Gesual-
da, niece of the composer Carlo Gesualdo.
Special singers were hired to perform the
music, which is for one and two sopranos.
The extreme virtuosity of the pieces attests
to the skill of the hired performers. The
only surviving original print of this volume
was destroyed during World War II, but a hand
copy by Alfred Einstein and Arno Reichert
provided the basis for a modern edition,
printed in 1957 as Volume 13 of the Smith
College Archives Series, edited by Vernon
Gotwals and Philip Keppler.

Quagliati (c.1555 - 1628) was born into a
noble family in Chioggia and settled in Rome
in 1574, where he lived the rest of his life.
He was organist at S. Maria Maggiore, served
the wealthy Ludovisi family, and was ac-

claimed as one of the finest keyboard players
in Rome. Active in the Counter-Reformation,
he was a respected composer of both sacred
and secular music, and wrote a short opera,
"Il Carro di fedelta"(1606).

Rontani, Raffaello. *Le Varie musiche ... a
     una due e tre voci per cantare nel
     Clavicembolo, et Chitarrone, Libro
     Primo*. Florence, 1614.

     *Le Varie musiche a una a due,
          e tre voci. Per cantare
          nel Gravicembalo, overo,
          nella Tiorba, et altri
          stromenti simili
          ... Libro Secondo*. Rome,
          1618.

     *Le varie musiche ... a una et
          due voci per cantare nel
          Cimbalo, o in altri
          stromenti simili con
          l'alfabeto per la Chitar-
          ra in quelle più a
          proposito per tale
          stromento. Libro Ter-
          zo*. Rome, 1619.

     *Varie musiche a una, e due
          voci ... per cantare nel
          Cimbalo, e nella Tiorba
          con l'alfabeto della
          Chitarra spagnola in
          quelli più a proposito
          per tale instromen-
          to. Libro Quarto*. Rome,
          1620.

> *Varie musiche a una e due voci
> per cantare nel Cimbalo,
> e nella Tiorba, con
> l'alfabeto della Chitarra
> spagnola in quelli più a
> proposito per tale in-
> stromento. Libro Quin-
> to.* Rome, 1620.

> *Le varie musiche ... A una, et
> due voci per cantare nel
> Cimbalo, o in altri
> stromenti simili. Libro
> Sesto.* Rome, 1622.

Works for solo voice dominate Rontani's six
collections, and he wrote in a variety of
musical styles, as well as for male and
female performers. The second collection is
more virtuosic than book I. Book III features two works in the style of ornamented
recitative, a very florid bass solo, and the
use of bass patterns. A copy of book IV was
unavailable to us, but it probably contains
works similar to those found in the earlier
collections. Book V, in the Newberry Library
volume along with book II (the second edition
of 1623), has an important dedication to *virtuosi* -- male and female -- and the virtuosic
works feature written-out trills and the use
of the *trillo* ornament. Compositions on bass
patterns reappear in book VI, combined with
some highly ornamented writing.

Rontani (? - 1622) was born in Florence and
first served the Medici family. His Florentine background is evident in his solos in
the style of ornamented recitative. By the
publication date of his second book, he was
working in Rome as *maestro di cappella* at
S. Giovanni dei Florentini. The posthumous
second printings of several collections in

Rome indicate his popularity as a Roman composer.

Rossi, Salomone. *Madrigaletti a due voci per cantar a doi soprani, overo tenori.* Venice, 1628.

This collection was compiled for two sopranos, or for two tenors, a popular means of publishing ensemble music so it would be marketable to a wider audience. All the pieces are written with treble clef, with only a few in the tenor clef, and in spite of the title, the last four pieces are for three voices. The music is in the north Italian style, and some pieces are quite long.

Rossi (c.1570 - c.1630) lived in Mantua and had strong connections with the Gonzaga court, although his Jewish faith apparently prevented him from advancements. His sister was a *virtuosa,* known only as Madama Europa. She performed at the Mantuan court and this collection was probably composed with her skills in mind. Rossi was an important figure in the development of the trio sonata, with its prominent upper voices over a supporting bass; these same textures are exhibited in his music for *virtuose.*

Rovetta, Giovanni. *Madrigali concertati a 2.3.4. et uno a sei voci, et due Violini. Con un Dialogo nel fine, et una Cantata a voce sola.* Venice, 1629.

Madrigali concertati, a due e

> *tre, voci, et altri a cinque, sei, et otto con due Violini et nel fine una Cantata a quattro.* Venice, 1640.
>
> *Madrigali concertati a due, tre, e quattro voci.* Venice, 1645.

Rovetta's three books of *Madrigali concertati*, published over a sixteen year time span, present some fine examples of virtuosic duets and trios for male and female voices. Book I contains a majority of duets for two tenors, written in contrasting sections of recitative style and virtuosic passages in 16th notes. At times, the *basso continuo* takes on an integral melodic role by imitating motives from the vocal lines. Book II favors larger vocal forces concerted with two violins. Book III, dedicated to Cavalli, returns to the duets and trio style of book I. The soprano takes on a more important role here with works for two sopranos as well as soprano and bass. In the later duets, the bass voice achieves a marked separation from the *basso continuo* line. The trios are not in the Roman three-voice texture, but rather are for *canto*, tenor and bass.

Rovetta (c.1595 - 1668) spent his entire life not only in Venice, but in the employ of S. Marco. He succeeded Alessandro Grandi as vice *maestro di cappella*, serving under Monteverdi. Rovetta's madrigals show the influence of the virtuosic writing style of Monteverdi's late books of madrigals. Rovetta became *maestro di cappella* after Monteverdi's death.

Sabbatini, Pietro Paolo. *Canzoni Spirituali a una, e due et a tre voci da cantarsi ... All'illustrissima, et eccellentissima signora principessa D. Anna Maria Cesi Peretti.* Rome, 1640.

This collection is entirely for one, two, and three sopranos, on spiritual texts, and dedicated to Anna Maria Cesi Peretti, the dedicatee of Quagliati's *Affetti amorosi spirituali*(1617). She evidently married later in life; while it is not known whether she performed professionally after she left S. Lucia, Sabbatini's dedication suggests that she was still a reputable singer. The music is not typically Roman, but falls more into the north Italian tradition. The final piece, a dialogue for three women, is the most ornate and difficult work in the collection.

Sabbatini (c.1600 - c.1657) spent his life in Rome, first as a singer and later as a professor of music. He published other collections of madrigals and sacred texts for one, two, and three sopranos as late as 1657.

Sances, Giovanni Felice. *Cantade ... a doi voci.* Venice, 1633.

The first large cycle, with seven *parti*, is a cantata for soprano, or soprano and bass. The rest of the collection is devoted to pieces for one and two sopranos, in the north Italian style. Though these works are labelled *cantade*, they highlight the differences in musical style between the early

cantata and music for *virtuose*, but also il-
luminate ways in which the cantata was initially dependent upon repertory for *virtuose*.

Sances (c.1600 - 1679) was born in Rome, but
resided in Vienna after 1636. While in Rome,
he was a composer, singer, and teacher, and
published numerous collections of chamber
music. He was one of the first composers to
employ the term *cantata*, though he applied it
to both through-composed and strophic pieces.

Strozzi, Barbara. *Il Primo Libro de'
Madrigali ... a due, tre, quattro, e cinque
voci*. Venice, 1644.

It is interesting that as late as 1644, one
of Venice's most gifted *virtuose* would still
publish a book of madrigals -- a genre that
had virtually died out elsewhere in Italy.
This collection offers nine pieces for two
voices, three pieces for three voices, four
works for four voices, and five pieces for
five voices. There are four madrigals for
two sopranos, in the north Italian style,
with an even balance between ornamentation
and slower-moving passages; there are also
two pieces for soprano and alto, and soprano
and tenor, which follow the north Italian
tradition. There is one madrigal for soprano
and bass which is more in the Roman style,
with emphasis on continuous embellishment.
The works for three voices also represent
both styles, with one piece for three
sopranos in the north Italian tradition, and
two pieces for two sopranos and bass. Barbara Strozzi was evidently quite familiar
with the "singing ladies" traditions of Rome
and northern Italy, and this collection

demonstrates a remarkable synthesis of the
two. One of the last collections of music
for *virtuose* to be published, it seems fitting that the music was composed by one of
the most gifted women in the early Baroque
period. Strozzi also published collections
of cantatas and arias in 1651 and 1654 which
include some pieces in the tradition of the
virtuosa. A selection of her works will be
published by Ellen Rosand in the near future.

Barbara Strozzi (1619 - 1664), adopted
daughter of the poet Giulio Strozzi, was born
in Venice. He promoted Strozzi's singing
career by founding the Accademia degli
Unisoni, where Strozzi performed and served
as moderator in literary debates. She composed eight collections of music, and she was
probably one of the last to perform in the
tradition of the "singing ladies". She died
sometime after 1664; for further information,
see the appendix.

Ugoni, Francesco. *Giardinetto di ricreatione
    Canzoni, et Madrigali ... Ad instanza
    d'alcuni virtuosissimi spirti, et
    nobilissime creature ad una, due, tre,
    quatro et cinque voci*. Milan, 1616.

Each piece in this collection is dedicated to
a different person, although it is not known
whether these people were performers or admirers of music. The edition was published
in Milan, a city for which no evidence of a
virtuoso ensemble has been discovered.
However, the volume was dedicated to the
director of the Accademia de Novelli di
Codogno, and the title mentions *virtuosi*,
suggesting that the music was designed for

specific singers. The three women to whom
pieces were dedicated were Laura Maria Lughi,
Camilla Lughi, and Clara Cipelli. The music
favors the Roman tradition, with eleven
pieces for two sopranos and bass; there are
also two solos, two pieces for two voices,
and five four and five-voice madrigals.

Ugoni, whose dates are unknown, was a priest
and organist at the Collegiate church in
Maleo Lodigiano, near Milan. This collection
is his only surviving publication.

Veneri, Gregorio. *Li Varii Scherzi ... a una
        a due a tre voci*. Rome, 1621.

The music was evidently compiled for the
dedicatee, Signora Dorotea Delfinoni, whom
Veneri apparently taught and served. The
pieces are mainly for soprano solo, with two
pieces for two sopranos, and a final work for
two sopranos and bass, all in the Roman
tradition. The first five entries are cycles
with several *parti*, over repeated bass patterns, and with each section becoming more
ornate than the one before it.

Veneri (1602 - c.1631) lived in Rome; nothing
is known about his career, but a 1631
publication describes him as *maestro di cappella* at Prato.

Visconte, Domenico. *Il Primo Libro de Arie a
        una e due voci*. Venice, 1616.

The volume is all for one or two sopranos,

mainly in the north Italian tradition but
with some strophic variations in the Roman
tradition. There are nineteen solos, including one cycle, and four pieces for two
sopranos; the solos are vocally more demanding.

Visconte (? - 1626) was a composer and organist for the Florentine court and was married to Lucrezia, a court singer and
musician. These pieces may have been composed for her, though she is not mentioned in
the dedication. Visconte settled in Rome
around 1626, but died shortly after his arrival.

Vitali, Filippo. *Musiche ... a due tre, e sei
voci. Libro Primo.* Florence, 1617.

> *Musiche a una, e due voci ...
> Libro secondo.* Rome,
> 1618.

> *Musiche ... A una due et tre
> voci. Per cantare nel
> Cimbalo, o in altri
> stromenti simili con
> l'alfabeto per la Chitar-
> ra in quelle più a
> proposito per stromen-
> to. Libro Terzo.* Rome,
> 1620.

> *Varie Musiche ... Libro Quin-
> to.* Venice, 1625.

> *Concerto ... et altri generi
> di canti a 1. 2. 3. 4. 5.
> et 6. voci.* Venice, 1629.

In general Vitali's collections feature
solos, duets, and trios in a variety of voice
groupings and demonstrate a combination of
Roman and north Italian practices. Books I
and II single out the tenor voice in both two
and three-voice textures, though the one virtuosic solo from book I is for soprano. Book
III is found in the Newberry Library volume
and contains the least virtuosic music.
Varie Musiche contains much music in the
simple, strophic style, though the work
closes with a piece for three sopranos and
basso continuo. The *Concerto* volume contains
three-voice works in the Roman style and a
virtuosic solo on the *romanesca* bass.

Vitali (c.1580 - c.1653) lived in Florence
until 1631 when he went to Rome as a papal
singer. He may have composed music for his
own use.

RAFFAELLA - VITTORIA ALEOTTI (c.1570 - 1646) was one of many women who attained a professional career through her attachment to a religious order. Raffaella's name before entering the Ferrarese convent of S. Vito was Vittoria, which has led some scholars to maintain that the architect of the Este court, Giovanni Battista Aleotti, had two talented daughters. Raffaella became the *maestra di concerto* of the famous S. Vito instrumental ensemble, the *concerto grande*. She also assisted in other aspects of the convent's musical education.

Before entering the convent, Raffaella studied music with Alessandro Milleville and Ercole Pasquini and published a collection of four-voice madrigals, *Ghirlanda di Madrigali*, in 1593. After joining S. Vito, Raffaella's compositions consisted of sacred works probably for performance by her equally talented sisters within the convent. Her collection of motets, *Sacrae cantiones*, was published in 1593.

VITTORIA ARCHILEI (1550 - c.1620) was probably the most famous *virtuosa* of the generation following the original Ferrarese *concerto delle donne*, and her singing career encompassed activities as both a virtuoso soloist and as a member of ensembles cast in the original tradition of the "three singing ladies." Originally from Rome and nicknamed "La Romanina", Archilei spent most of her life in the employ of the Medici family,

first in Rome and then in Florence, along
with her husband, Antonio, who was also a
singer and lutenist. Vittoria Archilei was a
member of the Florentine *concerto* of Grand
Duke Francesco, and continued in the employ
of Grand Duke Ferdinando after Francesco's
death in 1587. Archilei was one of the leading lights of the Medici musical establishment and participated in all their court
spectacles and celebrations. In the *intermezzo*, *La Pellegrina*, performed in 1589 on
the occasion of Ferdinando de Medici's marriage to Christine of Lorraine, Archilei accompanied herself on the lute and improvised
elaborate ornamentation on a solo composed
especially for her by Emilio de'Cavalieri.
Though in the employ of the Florentine
Medicis, Archilei managed to retain her Roman
ties and performed as a member of the Roman
concerto formed under the patronage of the
Orsini family in 1588, after the demise of
the Florentine *concerto* under Grand Duke Ferdinando.

Many composers made references to Archilei's
talent and ability in dedications to their
works, including Giulio Caccini, who knew her
talents from the Florentine *concerto* which he
directed and accompanied, Jacopo Peri, in his
dedication to *L'Euridice*, and Sigismondo
d'India, in his *Le Musiche* of 1609. All
three composers were proud to claim that Archilei had favored their music by performing
it. The writer Giustiniani in his *Discorso
sopra la Musica*(1628) credited Archilei posthumously with originating a new kind of singing for women and helping to spread this virtuosic style throughout Italy.

CATERINA ASSANDRA (fl.c.1609 - 1622) was

another female composer whose compositions
reflect her religious lifestyle. Assandra
belonged to the convent of S. Agata near
Milan, and her only surviving collection,
Motetti, her opus 2, is a book of motets for
two or three voices and *basso continuo*,
published in 1609. Single motets by her appeared in two other religious anthologies,
Siren coelestis and *Promptuarii musicus concentus ecclesiasticos*, published in 1616 and
1622, respectively.

AVOGADRI, sisters (fl.1589). According to
Anthony Newcomb's research, several Avogadri
sisters were members of a second and rival
concerto delle donne at the Ferrarese court,
whose patroness was Duke Alfonso's sister
Lucrezia, Duchess of Urbino. Evidently
Lucrezia, somewhat jealous of her sister-in-
law, felt slighted that she did not have her
own female ensemble. She formed a personal
concerto delle donne which was performing by
the late 1580s, and Duke Alfonso was
obligated to attend performances of both
groups held in the chambers of their respec-
tive Duchesses. It is unclear whether there
were two or three performing Avogadri
sisters, and little else is known about their
musical careers.

LEONORA (1611 - 1670) and CATERINA (1613 -
c.1670) BARONI were the two talented
daughters of the well-known mezzo-soprano,
Adriana Basile and her Neapolitan husband
Muzio Baroni. Leonora, the eldest, was born
shortly after her mother arrived in Mantua
from Naples, and Caterina was born two years
later. Duke Vincenzo Gonzaga had made con-

siderable efforts to acquire Basile's services for his professional musical staff, and
she was one of his most respected and highly
paid court members. Her two daughters were
accorded the benefits of a court up-bringing,
including education and musical training and
were doubtless present at numerous musical
events of the court.

Leonora achieved great acclaim as a soprano,
and some sources suggest that she eventually
surpassed her mother in vocal abilities. Her
mother was her primary teacher and manager
and evidently favored Leonora over the less-
gifted Caterina. Basile left the Mantuan
court abruptly in 1624 and returned with her
two daughters to Naples. Three years later,
at age 16, Leonora made her successful
professional debut in that city. In 1630,
she appeared in Genoa and Florence, and then
she and Caterina settled with their mother in
Rome, where they worked under the patronage
of the Rospigliosi family. Leonora married
Giulio Castellani in 1640; she was nearly 30
at the time, and the couple never had
children, suggesting that her professional
career may have been the dominant aspect of
her life.

In 1644, Leonora was offered a contract in
Paris by the Queen Regent of France, Anne of
Austria. While Leonora's voice was praised,
the Italian-style virtuoso music was not
popular in Paris at that time, and Leonora
returned shortly thereafter to Rome. She
continued to perform and hold chamber concerts until her death in 1670. The career of
Caterina is less well documented, although it
is known that she performed in ensembles with
Leonora and her mother.

ADRIANA BASILE (c.1580 - c.1640) began her
career in Naples, where she was recognized as
an outstanding mezzo-soprano and a gifted instrumentalist, especially on the harp and
Spanish guitar. Since Naples did not have a
secular virtuoso performing group of singers
during Adriana's youth, she probably received
her musical training at a convent. An
anthology of sacred madrigals, *Tempio Armonico*, published in 1599 by Giovenale Ancina, referred to a group of musical nuns at
the Neapolitan convent of S. Martino. The
founder of the convent, Sister Orsola Benincasa, was evidently responsible for the musical training of her charges. The convent
flourished during the decade 1590-1600 when
Adriana could have received instruction, so
it is quite probable that she was at some
time affiliated with S. Martino.

By 1608, Adriana was married to the
Neapolitan Muzio Baroni, and her musical
skills had already gained her considerable
attention. Throughout that year Duke Vincenzo Gonzaga of Mantua engaged in lengthy
negotiations to secure her for his court. He
finally agreed to numerous conditions, including a salary which exceeded that of court
composer Claudio Monteverdi, but it was not
until 1610 that Adriana left for Mantua,
stopping to perform in Rome and Florence on
the way. Susan Parisi's research shows that
Basile's professional success and status in
Mantua were remarkable. A Mantuan recruiting
agent wrote that Adriana knew more than 300
songs in Italian and Spanish from memory, and
that she could sing all kinds of madrigals
with such confidence that no singer could ex-
cel her. Parisi's research also uncovered
details about Basile's salary. In 1611 she
received 2000 *scudi*, plus an additional 1000
scudi in jewels, clothing and furnishings.

This income was decreased over her years of
service, but she was always one of the best
paid court musicians, earning as much as ten
times the amount paid to Monteverdi. Just
before her death in 1612, Duke Vincenzo Gonzaga conferred upon her and her husband a
feudal barony of Piancerreto in Monferrato,
which further increased her assets and income. The Duke also awarded dowries to her
two sisters, Margherita and Vittoria, and her
two brothers were made gentlemen of the
court. There is some evidence that her
sisters performed ensemble music with Basile
at the court.

Although Monteverdi must have envied Basile's
considerable salary, several of his surviving
letters attest to her musical excellence and
describe her solo and ensemble performances.
He also suggested that she was a competent
composer, and surviving letters and documents
of the Mantuan court, described by Ellen
Rosand in her research on Barbara Strozzi,
note that Basile was asked to send her better
compositions to the Grand Duke of Tuscany.
She was also successful under Duke Vincenzo's
successors, his sons Francesco and Ferdinando. Francesco ruled only briefly, but Basile
travelled with Duke Ferdinando's retenue in
1618 to perform in Florence and Rome. In
1623, she went to Venice with the Duke and
Duchess for a celebration in their honor.
She was recognized in Venice with the
publication of a collection of poems by leading writers, *Il teatro delle glorie*,
presented to her during the visit.

After her Venetian triumph, she suddenly left
the Mantuan court and returned to Naples.
Despite frequent requests, she never returned
to Mantua, and no specific reason has been
found for her hasty departure. In 1633,

Basile settled in Rome with her two daughters, Leonora and Caterina Baroni. She trained them both as professional singers, and especially Leonora enjoyed considerable success. The three women were sponsored by the Rospigliosi family and performed together in chamber concerts until Basile's death around 1640.

ORSOLA BENINCASA (fl.1599) was a founder and member of the Neapolitan convent of S. Martino and according to Giovenale Ancina's dedication to *Tempio Armonico* (1599) was also the founder of a famed singing group made up of convent members. It is likely that Benincasa was herself a singer and may have been responsible for other musical activities and musical training at the convent.

LAURA BOVIA (fl.1580 - 1590) was a member of the Florentine *concerto delle donne*, the first successful imitation of the famed Ferrarese ensemble. Formed under the direction of Grand Duke Francesco around 1584, the Florentine *concerto* included Lucia Caccini and Vittoria Archilei and was directed and accompanied by Giulio Caccini. From Bologna, Bovia initially made a name for herself as a virtuoso singer while attached to the Bolognese convent of S. Lorenzo, which further testifies to the importance of religious orders in training women for careers as professional musicians. The Florentine *concerto delle donne* flourished until Francesco's death in 1587, and it was later disbanded under Grand Duke Ferdinando. Little is known of Bovia after that, and she may have returned to her convent to pursue her singing career.

FRANCESCA CACCINI (1587 - 1640) was the
eldest daughter of the composer and poet
Giulio Caccini and his first wife, the singer
Lucia. Carolyn Raney's dissertation on Francesca Caccini's *Primo Libro* (1618) (previously cited) sheds light on her career and her
relationship to the *concerto delle donne* in
Florence. Caccini was born in Florence on
September 18, 1587 and worked there
throughout her life. She was extremely ver-
satile: although especially heralded for her
virtuoso singing, she was an accomplished
poetess, played the lute, guitar and
harpsichord, composed and succeeded in having
some of her works published, and she taught.
Nicknamed "La Cecchina", she was a favorite
at the Florentine court for much of her life.

Since Caccini's parents were both prominent
musicians in Florence, her training was
largely supplied by them. But she was also
exposed to the wide variety of musical events
and performers that Florence sponsored during
her formative years. Her father Giulio was
primarily responsible for the first Florentine *concerto delle donne*. Established
around 1584, shortly after he and other
Florentine delegates visited the Ferrarese
carnival and heard the original *concerto
delle donne*, the Florentine ensemble was
coached and accompanied by Giulio. His first
wife Lucia was a member, as were the Roman
Vittoria Archilei, and the Bolognese Laura
Bovia. Francesca Caccini was born just
before the death of Grand Duke Francesco de
Medici in October of 1587. His brother Ferdinando succeeded him and immediately altered
all musical establishments including the *con-*

certo. Only Vittoria Archilei was main-
tained, and Giulio and Lucia were not in
favor for several years; Lucia was never rehired by the Florentine court. Ferdinando
brought several singers from Rome, probably
with the assistance of Archilei, and charge
of the womens' ensemble and other musical
events was given over to Emilio de'Cavalieri.
Francesca sometimes performed with Archilei
and the other Roman singers, and it seems
likely that much of the virtuoso ensemble
music performed by Ferdinando's ensemble was
of the Roman style. So Francesca's background included both her father's adherence
to the Ferrarese *concerto* format, and the
Roman admiration for ornate *passaggi* and
repeated bass patterns; both influences are
evident in her compositions.

Francesca Caccini made her first appearance
as a singer at the wedding of Maria de Medici
and Henry IV, King of France, in 1600, when
she was only 13 years old. The King wanted
her to remain in Paris, but the Tuscan court
refused and she returned to Florence where
she became a paid court member in 1607. By
1614, she was receiving 20 *scudi* a year, far
from the 1000 *scudi* Mantua paid Adriana
Basile, but making Francesca one of the
highest paid musicians in Florence. She frequently performed as a soloist, but for special festivities Ferdinando engaged Vittoria
Archilei, and Francesca's sister Settimia
joined them to form a *concerto*.

Caccini married a singer, Giovanni Battista
Signorini Malaspina, and the two made several
tours to Italian cities. She started her own
school of pupils, whom she apparently taught
to sing and compose. Her followers became
known as her *scuola*, noted for their music
and poetry, and probably responsible for much

of the entertainment at intellectual gatherings.

Caccini was also successful as a poet and
composer. She collaborated with the poet
Michelangelo Buonarroti the younger, in songs
and court entertainments; three of the latter, though they do not survive, were apparently large-scale works. One of these, *Il
ballo delle Zigane*, was set to music by Francesca and performed at the Pitti Palace
during the 1615 carnival. She is best remem-
bered for *La liberazione di Ruggiero*, first
performed in Florence in 1625 to celebrate
the visit of the future King Wladislaw IV of
Poland. It eventually became the first
Italian opera to be given in its entirety
outside Italy, when it was performed in Warsaw in 1682. The work is full of choruses
for three singing ladies, or *damigelle*. Caccini also published a book of madrigals, *Il
primo Libro*, in 1618.

Caccini's first husband died in 1626. She
may have re-married, since a document suggests that at her death she was the wife of a
senator. Her local fame diminished during
her last years, though the reverence of her
students was in large part responsible for
preserving her name and music.

LUCIA CACCINI (fl.1570 - 1606) was Giulio
Caccini's first wife and the mother of the
famous *virtuose* Francesca and Settimia.
Lucia Caccini was a singer in her own right
and performed with the Florentine *concerto
delle donne*, styled on the original Ferrarese
ensemble, which included the sopranos Vittoria Archilei and Laura Bovia. Her husband,
Giulio Caccini, coached and directed the

Florentine *concerto*, and it flourished from 1584 - 1587 under the patronage of Grand Duke Francesco de Medici. However after his death in 1587, the *concerto* was disbanded by the succeeding Grand Duke Ferdinando, and Caccini was never rehired by the Medici court. Caccini later performed as a member of the Caccini family consort which performed at the French court in 1604-05. Lucia Caccini, as well as her husband, may have helped train and prepare their daughters for their careers as professional singers.

SETTIMIA CACCINI (1591 - c.1638), nicknamed *La Flora*, was the youngest daughter of Giulio and Lucia Caccini and the younger sister of Francesca. While her sister eventually became the more famous of the musical sisters, their parents considered them to be equally talented and encouraged both of them in their education and musical pursuits. Like Francesca, Settimia grew up among the fine musicians and singing ladies of the Florentine court, was trained by her parents, and received a good education. She evidently established herself as a singer at an early age, for she made court appearances with Francesca while still a child. For two years, while she was 13 and 14, she toured with her family in Paris although the extent of her performing is not known. When she and her family returned to Florence, she continued to perform there, though without professional status.

Her first paid performance came in Mantua, where she sang the role of Venus in the first production of Monteverdi's opera *Arianna* (now lost). She married Alessandro Ghivizzani in 1609, and together they entered the service

of the Florentine court with professional
status in November of 1609. Ghivizzani was
also a singer and composer, and a few secular
songs with *basso continuo* by Caccini and
Ghivizzani survive in manuscript.

Caccini and her husband returned to Mantua in
1612 where Caccini was in demand. She seemed
to follow her husband's career afterwards,
moving to Lucca and Parma during the 1620s
where Ghivizzani found employment. Caccini
apparently had little difficulty finding
singing opportunities wherever she went. She
was especially lauded in a performance of
Monteverdi's *Mercurio e Marte* in 1628, which
inaugurated the Teatro Farnese at Parma.
After her husband died in 1632, Caccini
returned to Florence and re-entered the court
service there in 1636. Although the name
Settimia Ghivizzani occurs in the court accounts through 1660, it is generally assumed
that Settimia died around 1638 and that the
references are to a daughter.

Caccini frequently performed in virtuoso ensembles with her sister in Florence. Her
singing career apart from Florence seemed to
depend upon her location and upon her husband's circumstances. She was a gifted
soloist as was Francesca, but evidently she
put her own professional goals after her husband's professional success. Contemporary
descriptions of her singing suggest that she
was considered equal to her famous sister,
but because she moved frequently with her
husband, she was not as likely to establish a
lasting reputation.

FRANCESCA CAMPANA (fl.1629 - 1665) was a
Roman singer, composer, and spinet player.

She appears to have been somewhat well-known
and regarded for her talents in her day.
Only one publication by Campana survives,
Arie a una, due e tre voci, of 1629, which
she probably composed for her own use as a
performer.

ANNA MARIA CESI(PERETTI) (fl.1617 - 1640)
came from the prominent Marchesi d'Oliveto
branch of the noble Roman Cesi family. She
professed to have been born around 1608, but
was probably born about ten years earlier
since she was an acclaimed singer by 1617.
Cesi was a member of the convent of S. Lucia
in Selice. Since her family was not lacking
in funds for a suitable dowry, it is likely
that Cesi and her family chose the convent
for its educational and musical benefits;
Cesi later left the convent and was married
to a member of the Peretti family.

Cesi brought special acclaim to S. Lucia and
its musical nuns. In 1617, the composer Paolo Quagliati dedicated his *Affetti amorosi
spirituali* to her. His student, Pietro della
Valle, wrote in his *Della musica dell'età
nostra*(1640) that the nuns at S. Lucia were
the marvel of Rome. Although he did not mention her name specifically, he noted that
"Everyone knows how much renown the nun at
Santa Luccia in Selice has", and it is
generally accepted that Cesi was the intended
recipient of his praise. Before his death in
1628, Quagliati left instructions that his
spinet should be donated to the nuns at
S. Lucia, another sign of his admiration.

In 1640, another Roman composer, Pietro Sabbatini, dedicated his book of *Canzoni
spirituali a una, due e tre voci* to Cesi, who

was then married as is suggested in Sabbatini's preface. Although no documents survive that describe her career after she left
S. Lucia, Sabbatini's dedication infers that
Cesi was still a formidable Roman singer in
1640, at which time she was probably nearing
fifty years of age.

ISABELLA COLLEATA (fl.1623) appears to have
been the leading female singer at the court
of Savoy in Turin during the tenure of Filippo Albini as court composer. Albini's
Musicali Concenti(1623) specifically mentions
Colleata's performances of two works and
dedicates a third composition to her. The
opening work in the collection, "La Notte",
composéd in honor of the Duke Carlo
Emanuelle's birthday, is an elaborate and
highly virtuosic composition in four stanzas
which Colleata premiered at the birthday festivities for the Duke. The dedication to "La
Notte" describes Colleata as a *Cantatrice
Virtuossissima* [sic] e *musica.* A
second work, "L'ogistilla Maga", part of a
balletto, again mentions Colleata's performance. The third composition dedicated to
Colleata is "Dolcissimo Uscignulo", a simple
aria spirituale. Other virtuosic works in
the collection were undoubtedly written with
Colleata in mind. Though two other women,
Margherita Maroni and Isabella Pongini, are
mentioned in this publication, they appear to
have been only dedicatees since no mention is
made of their musical ability.

LIVIA D'ARCO (fl.1579 - 1598) was first a
member of Duchess Margherita Gonzaga
d'Este's personal entourage before receiving

enough training to became a full performing member of the original Ferrarese *concerto delle donne.* D'Arco came from a minor noble Mantuan family and also performed on the viola da gamba.

ANNA GUARINI (fl.1590 - 1598), the second soprano brought to the Este court to form the original Ferrarese *concerto delle donne,* was the daughter of the poet Giovanni Battista Guarini. She was also known as a lutenist. Her career as a professional musician was cut short by her murder in 1598 by her jealous husband, Ercole Trotti.

CATERINA MARTINELLI (c.1589 - 1608), nick-named "La Romanina" in honor of her Roman birthplace, was already known for her vocal accomplishments before she arrived at the Mantuan court of Duke Vincenzo Gonzaga in 1603. By that time the Mantuan court employed many famous male and female *virtuosi* and Martinelli took her place as one of the jewels in Vincenzo's musical establishment. She lived as member of the Claudio Monteverdi household and may have studied with Montever-di's wife Claudia, who was herself a court singer. Martinelli took an active part in the operatic life of Mantua and sang the role of Venus in Marco da Gagliano's *Le Dafne,* performed in 1608. She was to have sung the lead role in Monteverdi's *L'Arianna,* but died of smallpox before the performance took place. Monteverdi, who considered Martinelli a member of his own family, mourned her death, as did the entire Mantuan court. Mon-teverdi later wrote a madrigal cycle in her honor, *Lagrime d'amanti al sepulcro dell'amata* found in book VII of his madrigals, published in 1614, and Duke Vincenzo endowed memorial Requiem masses. A court decree published after her premature death described her as an "extraordinary singer".

ISABELLA MALESPINI MASTIANI (fl.1617) was a member of a leading Pisan family and studied music and performed with the composer Vicenzo Calestani, who dedicated his *Madrigali et Arie* of 1617 to her. It is unclear whether she was a true *virtuosa* or merely a trained amateur performer.

TARQUINIA MOLZA (c.1542 - 1617) came from Modena and was probably the second most famous member of the original Ferrarese *concerto delle donne* after Laura Peverara. Molza was an accomplished singer, instrumentalist, and poet, and like Peverara, was the focus of poetic and musical accolades; in particular, the philosopher Francesco Patrizi dedicated several works to her between the years of 1577 and 1581. Molza was banished from the Este court in 1589 because of her illicit love affair with the court composer Giaches de Wert. She returned to Modena and continued her career as a performing musician, attracting a new circle of admirers and patrons. She was later given the honor of Roman citizenship, the first woman to receive this distinction, and was buried in the Modena Cathedral after her death in 1617. The Latin inscription on her tomb (published in Durante and Martelloti's *Cronistoria del Concerto*) reads:

A life of such knowledge
as that of Tarquinia Mol-
za, falls into the common
grave. Died 8 August,
1617, her life spanned 74
years.

CLAUDIA DA CATTANEIS MONTEVERDI (fl.1590 -
1607) was employed by the illustrious musical
court of the Mantuan Gonzaga family. She was
already a court singer before her husband arrived in 1591 to become a court instrumentalist, and her marriage to him followed in
1599. Little further is known about her
career due to her premature death, though she
may have instructed another famous Mantuan
singer, Caterina Martinelli. Martinelli
lived as a member of the Monteverdi household
following her arrival in Mantua in 1603 until
her death in 1608. Since all of Claudio Monteverdi's works for *virtuose* post-date
Claudia's death by over a decade, it is unlikely that he composed anything especially
for her. His earlier five-voice madrigal
collections which do reflect the influence of
the *concerto* were probably not meant for
Claudia either, as she is never mentioned as
a singer in the select Mantuan *concerto*.

LUCREZIA ORSINA (fl.c.1623) was a composer
and a member of the Bolognese convent of
S. Christina. Her compositions, consisting
of sacred works for a small number of voices
and *basso continuo*, were published as *Componimenti Musicali di motetti concertanti* in
1623. Again her compositions were undoubtedly written with the needs and talents of her
own convent in mind.

ISABELLA and LUCIA PELLIZZARI (fl.1580 - 1600) were born and trained in Vicenza and were part of Duke Vincenzo of Mantua's *concerto delle donne* when he arrived in Ferrara for the carnival in April of 1589. Anthony Newcomb suggests that the other members of Vincenzo's *concerto* at this time were Catterina Romana and Lucrezia Urbani, though Susan Parisi maintains that such a foursome could not have performed together until 1603. The Pellizzari sisters, members of a musical family in Vicenza, appeared together with their brother Antonio in the Accademia Olimpica in Vicenza; all three were apparently members of the academy in 1581-82. Duke Guglielmo, Vincenzo Gonzaga's father, heard the ladies while on a trip to their hometown, and he also noted that they were skilled in playing the cornet and trombone. Vincenzo either heard of the sisters from his father, or was present in Vicenza for one of their performances, as he hired them for the Mantuan court as soon as the city's budget came under his control. According to Susan Parisi's research, five members of the Pellizzari family were at one time on Duke Vincenzo's payroll; it is not known how long Isabella and Lucia remained in service at Mantua, or if they subsequently performed at other courts.

LAURA PEVERARA (fl.1580 - 1601) was a member of the original Ferrarese *concerto delle donne* and throughout its existence, she was the *concerto's* most famous and celebrated member. Poets, composers, and court correspondents alike extolled her various

talents and abilities. Peverara was the
recipient of many special dedications in particular the two musical anthologies, *Il Lauro
secco*(1582) and *Il Lauro verde*(1583), compiled by the poet Torquato Tasso, a great admirer of Peverara. She continued her singing
career in Ferrara after the dissolution of
the Este court in 1598 and had a profound influence on the development and popularity of
virtuoso female performers.

MADAMA EUROPA (ROSSI) (fl.1610 - 1620) was
the sister of the widely acclaimed composer
Salomone Rossi. Rossi, born in Mantua near
1570, worked in the Mantuan court for several
years until his death in 1628. He and his
sister, whose actual name is not recorded,
had strong connections with the Gonzaga
court. Their Jewish heritage prevented them
from advancing in court status or receiving
significant salaries and was probably why
Europa's name and career were not well documented in Mantuan court records. Her performing years would have overlapped with
Adriana Basile's and with the most productive
years for the Mantuan *concerto delle donne*.
While Europa probably performed at court festivities and acted in a local troupe, she was
probably not a member of the Duke's professional *concerto delle donne*.

CATTERINA ROMANA (fl.1589) was identified by
Anthony Newcomb as a member of the Mantuan
concerto delle donne which may have included
the Pellizzari sisters and Lucrezia Urbani.
The Mantuan *concerto* was formed under the
patronage of Duke Vincenzo Gonzaga, long an
admirer of the original Ferrarese ensemble,

and was performing by the late 1580s. According to Giustiniani in *Discorso sopra la
musica*(1618), the Mantuan *concerto delle
donne* rivaled its Ferrarese model and the
closely connected courts, related by marriage, held performance competitions between
the two rival *concerti*. Romana's surname indicates a Roman heritage or birthplace,
shared with other noted *virtuose* such as Vittoria Archilei and Caterina Martinelli, and
may further indicate that Rome possessed special facilities or convents which trained
professional female performers.

GIOVANNA SANCIA (fl.1599), a Spaniard, was a
member of the Neapolitan convent of S. Martino which was famed for its singing sisters
under the direction of sister Orsola Benincasa. The dedication to Giovenale Ancina's
Tempio Armonico(1599), which mentions the
convent's musical activities, comments in
particular on Sancia's talents and refers to
her as "a neapolitan siren".

BARBARA STROZZI (1619 - c.1665), often
referred to as *virtuosissima cantatrice* , was
well-known in Venice for both her singing and
composing. Recent research by Ellen Rosand
has uncovered much information about her life
and career. Strozzi was born in Venice, the
illegitimate daughter of Isabella Griega.
Strozzi's father was probably Giulio Strozzi,
a figure of considerable importance in
Venetian cultural life. He founded and supported numerous academies, was a prolific
poet and dramatist, and provided libretti for
several operas performed in Venice during the
1630s and 1640s. Isabella was apparently his

servant and mistress for several years, and
named as his sole heir in an early will.
Barbara assumed his surname and was raised in
the Strozzi household and accorded all the
privileges of a daughter. Giulio provided
her with excellent musical training, arranged
for her to study composition with Cavalli,
promoted her professional career, and his
status granted her opportunities that probably would have been denied to other women.

By 1634, Giulio Strozzi had arranged for Barbara to sing informally at his home, where
she was heard by other members of the musical
community. The composer Nicolò Fontei was
inspired to write two volumes of songs for
her, published in 1635 and 1636 and entitled
Bizzarrie Poetiche. By 1637, Giulio evidently decided that Strozzi's vocal talents
merited widespread attention. Venice did not
sponsor a *concerto delle donne* and apparently
neither the convent nor opera appealed to
her. So Giulio institutionalized her performances through the creation of the Accademia
degli Unisoni. She served as mistress of
ceremonies for debates on academic and
frivolous subjects and was expected to sing
and improvise songs on the daily topics for
debate. It is unlikely that she was paid for
her services. Although women were occasionally invited to attend academic meetings as special guests, they were not ad-
mitted to membership. But it was publically
acknowledged that Strozzi was the academy's
hostess, artist-in-residence, and guiding
spirit. She performed frequently and was
known throughout Venice for her excellent
singing. Although their names are not
recorded, other women were apparently brought
into the academy to sing with Strozzi and
provide ensemble entertainment.

Strozzi's determination to publish her own
compositions assumed a special significance
for her time. While other *virtuose* such as
Adriana Basile were known to have composed,
few women attempted to publish their works.
Strozzi's public stature as a composer distinguished her from her female counterparts.
She studied counterpoint with her father's
encouragement. After her father's death in
1652, Strozzi apparently tried to secure her
living through her music. She published
eight volumes of works for one, two, and
three voices; each was dedicated to a different dignitary, suggesting that Strozzi
sought a permanent patron. Evidently she was
unsuccessful in this attempt, though her
music forms a significant part of early
Baroque vocal repertory. Her career survived
her father's by only a decade and nothing is
known about her activities after the publication of her eighth book of compositions in
1664.

Barbara Strozzi was probably one of the last
women to sing in the tradition of the
original *virtuosa*. Despite Venice's reputation for opera after 1640, Strozzi specialized only in solo and ensemble chamber music.
She performed privately with other sopranos
and distinguished herself from her peers only
in her efforts to publish her own works.
This effort was significant , and in spite of
the talent represented in her scores, she was
evidently not able to secure a place as a
professional composer. Yet she was perhaps
one of the most significant musicians of her
time: she heralded both the close of the
Renaissance-style virtuoso and the advent of
the Baroque solo performer.

LUCREZIA URBANI (fl.1589) was again identified by Anthony Newcomb as a member of the
Mantuan *concerto delle donne* of Duke Vincenzo
Gonzaga. She performed with other ensemble
members which included the Pellizzari sisters
and Catterina Romana. Little else is known
about her career or professional activities.
Since Giustiniani in his *Discorso sopra la
musica*(1618) implies that the Mantuan *concerto delle donne* came to rival its Ferrarese
model, Urbani must have been a competent and
highly trained *virtuosa*.

INDEX

Olivieri, Giuseppe, 67, 116-117
opera, 36-37, 43, 77-78, 81-82, 84-85,
   119-120, 140-142, 145-146, 150-152
Orlandi, Camillo, 117-118
ornamentation, 7, 11-14, 36, 43-44, 54, 56,
   58-60, 64-67, 74-76, 79-80, 91-92, 94-98,
   102-103, 105, 112-113, 117-118, 121,
   125-126, 131-132, 138-139
ornamented recitative, 79-80, 82, 92, 94-95,
   97-98, 102-104, 117-118, 121-122
Orsina, Lucrezia, 23-24, 147
Orsini family, 131-132
Ortiz, Diego, 59-60
Oxford, 27-28

Padua, 116
Palestrina, Giovanni, 54-55, 63-64
Paris, 134, 139, 141
Parisi, Susan, 30-31, 135-136, 148
Parma, 112, 142
Pasquini, Ercole, 21, 23, 60-61, 131
Patrizi, Francesco, 146
Pellizzari, Antonio, 148
Pellizzari, Isabella, 30-31, 148-150, 153
Pellizzari, Lucia, 30-31, 148-150, 153
Peri, Jacopo, 16-17, 77, 132
Pesaro, 106, 108
Petrarch, Francesco, 74-75, 110
Peverara, Laura, 9-11, 17-18, 146, 148-149
Pisa, 98, 146
Poland, 90, 140
Pongini, Isabella, 89, 144

Quagliati, Paolo, 23, 38, 41-42, 54, 56,
   118-120, 143

Raney, Carolyn, 97-98
Ravetto, Luiggi, 89
Reichert, Arno, 119
Rinuccini, Ottavio, 74-75